HIDDEN
TALENTS

HIDDEN TALENTS

Practical Tools and Inspirational Stories
to Unleash Higher Levels
of Leadership Performance

MARYANNE DIMARZO | AMY ACKER | RODICA CESLOV

Edited by M. Eileen Brown

ISBN: 978-0-578-58458-4

First Edition

For information about permission to reproduce selections from this book,
please contact Rights@hiddentalentsbook.com

For information about special discounts for bulk purchases, or for use in
corporate training, please contact Sales@HiddenTalentsBook.com

Visit HiddenTalentsBook.com

*Dedicated to one of the best human resources teams
ever assembled and to the exceptional company
where leaders chose to lead.*

*With appreciation to Barbara DiMarzo
for finishing touches.*

CONTENTS

PART ONE
TOOLS FOR LEADING INTO THE FUTURE

PART TWO
TOOLS FOR BUILDING CONNECTIONS THAT ADVANCE THE BUSINESS

INTRODUCTION

"I am not what happened to me. I am what I choose to become."

CARL JUNG

A few years ago, while we were leading a strategy session for a leadership team of a Fortune 500 company, we overheard a conversation that touched us. One of the vice presidents told a story about a company that, after making significant investments in leadership development, went on to enjoy increased growth and profitability. The story referenced a spin-off from a parent company, that had more success than anticipated and, in his opinion, accomplished what they did because of their commitment to leadership development. The more he talked, the more familiar the story sounded. It was our company, and his assessment was accurate. He either did not know, or he had forgotten about our work there. When we confirmed that his conclusion was correct, the agenda of the meeting switched to answering questions about our experience and how our work contributed to the results that nobody had anticipated. At that moment, we realized that we had to tell this story and to offer our practical advice and tools to help other leaders achieve higher levels of performance.

When Carl Jung said, "I am not what happened to me. I am what I choose to become," he asserted that we have options: we can choose fatalism, or we can choose "possibility." For those who believe that "they are what happened to them," we suggest that they chose a very narrow path for themselves; a way that depends on external forces and even the fates more than personal efforts. Those who believe that "they are what they choose to become," choose a more expansive view, the depth, and breadth of the choices available to each of us, including the choice to lead. Naturally, we, as leadership development practitioners, embrace the latter with all the freedom and possibility it offers. We have become crystal clear in our beliefs that we "choose to become" leaders — that leadership is a choice.

Earlier in our thinking, we may have doubted or even dismissed the wisdom of this premise for the more elaborate theories, platforms, models and tools that have trended in the field of leadership development through the years. We, too, were caught on that "hamster wheel," continually running after the next set of leadership competencies or performance management systems. We were almost always disappointed with the results of our efforts.

Many of us learned different models and tools to identify "strengths" and "weaknesses." Then "development areas" replaced "weaknesses" as less judgmental language became popular. We dissected individuals' leadership behaviors as if understanding the "parts" could help us truly understand the complicated dynamics of the "whole." Again, these efforts produced much activity but disappointing results.

Through the years, we grew to value two fundamental concepts. The first is that **perspective is decisive**. Our perspective on an issue determines the actions we take, and the performance levels we achieve.

The second concept is that human beings are born with access to all the tools needed in today's workplace and life and that we have more capability to develop **leadership prescriptions** for ourselves than we realize. Some of those tools are more practiced and natural than others, but even those less accessible or, what we refer to as *hidden talents*, are available for us to practice and develop.

This book explores these two fundamental concepts and how they open the door to all our talents — even those that are less visible to us. Each of the leaders in this book chose to change their perspective on what was possible from them to accomplish and chose to use their natural abilities and their *hidden talents* to effectively utilize their leadership tools to produce more powerful leadership outcomes. *They chose to lead, and they achieved higher levels of performance.*

Through the chapters of this book, we are going to introduce you to sixteen leaders who learned how to access their less familiar leadership tools and how they became skilled in their use. Faced with bona fide business problems, they taught themselves to reach into their toolkit, pick the right skill, and deliver the right results. Each of these leaders will be featured modeling one of the sixteen tools that we highlight throughout this book.

The tools we introduce in this book have stood the test of time. The examples cited here are from the early 2000s, and they remain the top areas recommended for development among our clients. They are even more relevant in today's fast-changing world in which new technologies are upending work as we know it because they help leaders develop clarity about the capabilities and skills they need to prepare their teams and their companies for the future. Our goal is to describe these tools in simple, concrete and behavior-based language that enables the readers to distinguish what areas of skill and expertise they can naturally call upon and what areas of their *hidden talents* they can call up with conscious effort and develop over time.

Between us, we have decades of experience with leadership development in the business and the non-profit world. As C-Suite officers and consultants, we have seen and continue to see the possibilities that open for leaders once they understand and embrace this perspective. Somehow, development becomes clear, within their reach and more comfortable to access.

Who will benefit from this book?

The book is packed with practical advice and tools to help anyone become a better leader at any leadership level. For beginning managers, the tools presented here can serve as a guide as they continue through their development journey. It also teaches them to lead from where they are (Chapter 3: *Listening for Possibilities*). For experienced leaders, the tools presented in the book can help them effectively pick the right skill and deliver the right results.

PERSPECTIVE IS DECISIVE

"The real voyage of discovery consists not in seeking new lands but in seeing with new eyes."

MARCEL PROUST

Amanda was a human resources vice president for a segment of the business. She was sometimes frustrated by what she saw as obstacles to doing her job well and blamed the business leaders for omitting her from their staff meetings. One of her peers suggested that she change her perspective from "they" will not give me the opportunity, to "I will create my opportunity." So, she did.

Different perspectives lead to different choices – and, those choices either limit or enhance our performance levels.

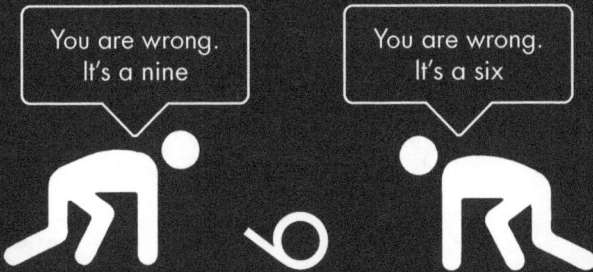

You are wrong. It's a nine

You are wrong. It's a six

That simple change in perspective opened her mind to some possible ideas. Amanda was already on the distribution list for the meeting agenda, so she could predict the topics that were under consideration. She began sending the meeting participants information and analysis that was relevant to their discussions. Slowly, the business leader started inviting her in for parts of the meeting. Amanda made sure that she actively and productively contributed to the talks. After a few weeks, she was invited to attend all the meetings.

Amanda changed her perspective, allowed herself to "hear" some new ideas, tried them, and reached new performance heights. It all starts with perspective.

LEADERSHIP PRESCRIPTIONS

"We become what we behold. We shape our tools and then our tools shape us."

MARSHALL MCLUHAN

Just as medical professionals write prescriptions for better health outcomes, leaders can write prescriptions for better performance levels. The leadership tools we present in this book can be applied using prescriptions that leaders at all levels can employ to advance their leadership skills and their careers.

We define a **leadership tool** as a set of talents used in combination to create a specific outcome, either personally or through others. Leadership tools require a carefully balanced blend of knowledge and experience, personality characteristics, and preferences plus leadership talents and skills to implement effectively. Further, we differentiate between a talent and a skill: *skill* is a talent that one has developed into a high degree of proficiency and, talent is an inborn ability to do something. Both are available for leaders who choose to uncover their "hidden talents" to enhance their leadership.

Let's return to Amanda's story. She had enough confidence in her knowledge and experience to see that her contributions would enhance the leadership team's decision process. She also accepted personal accountability to create her own opportunity to contribute and the courage to make herself vulnerable to the leadership team. Amanda then prescribed the actions that she could take to become a significant contributor to the discussions of the leadership team. She accepted the leadership challenge to "become what she chose to be" and, in doing so, increased her performance levels.

> ## PRESCRIPTION
>
> Amanda, HR VP
>
> Choose to remove barriers to higher performance levels:
>
> 1. Rely on your knowledge and experience and assume personal accountability.
>
> 2. Contribute thoughtful analysis on relevant meeting topics.
>
> 3. Be prepared to be called into meetings to explain the analysis.

Throughout this book, we describe several essential leadership tools in simple, concrete and behavior-based language that enables the reader to distinguish what areas of skill and expertise they can naturally call upon and what areas of their hidden talents they can call up with conscious effort and develop over time. We also consistently see that calling out these tools and naming them gives leaders access to a language that they become fluent in their conversations with one another about coaching and development.

The leaders highlighted in this book are real, and we frequently find remarkably similar challenges and choices facing many of our clients today — and similar successes when they have embraced these leadership tools.

HOW TO USE THIS BOOK

"Stories are the shortest distance between us and the truth. So, when we understand and uncover these stories, we gain the opportunity to understand that maybe we need a new story."

CHRIS CADE

The Stories: Why we tell them and how you can use them?

We use stories of real leaders throughout this book to describe the leadership tools that we present in action. Stories offer us a view of the change we seek and the challenges we face un-encumbered by our "voices of resistance." Stories allow us to look through the eyes of others who met similar situations and similar choices; and how they changed their perspectives and wrote new leadership prescriptions to achieve higher levels of performance. In short, the stories of these real leaders help our readers envision the success that they seek and create a new story for themselves.

> *We encourage you to envision yourself in these stories, to walk in the shoes of the individuals demonstrating these leadership tools, and to notice the linkage between the perspective they adopted, the prescription they designed and the performance they achieved. Reflect upon the elements of each leadership tool that are more natural fits for you and those that would take some focused attention and development to meet the outcomes you seek.*

"Four Times Four:" How is the book structured?

This book is divided into four parts, and each has four chapters. Each section describes the tools that will be presented in the following four chapters along with Coaching Tips, for each tool. Each chapter features a different leader using a separate leadership tool to solve a specific problem, to discover and develop their talents, including their hidden talents and a summary of the shift in their perspective, a leadership prescription and their new performance level. Additionally, each chapter describes the ineffective use of each tool through over or under-emphasis. Finally, each chapter will end with a "final tip" from the featured leader.

> *We encourage you to notice the descriptions of each tool when they are not used effectively — when they are over or underemphasized. Notice the examples of feedback other leaders have received when they use the tool ineffectively. Does any of the feedback sound familiar? If so, make a note of the associated coaching. We encourage you to read them all in order, but we recognize that some readers may want to focus on specific leadership tools that appear to address their most pressing needs.*

Tool Practice Sheets:
What development actions do you see?

Follow the tool practice sheets for the leadership tools that most resonate with you. *Download them at hiddentalentsbook.com/ToolPractice.* Use them to create a leadership tool inventory and development actions for yourself or others.

One final note

We wrote this book from multiple perspectives. When we offer coaching, we speak from "us to you," using first and second-person pronouns. When we share the stories of leaders, we speak "about them," we speak in the third person.

PART ONE:
TOOLS FOR LEADING INTO THE FUTURE

"Go back?" he thought. "No good at all! Go sideways? Impossible! Go forward? Only thing to do! On we go!"

R. R. TOLKIEN

One of the most daunting challenges that today's leaders face is how to effectively and intentionally lead others to a new and uncertain place. Think about it. The future is "uncharted" territory. Its paths are unclear; its dangers are ambiguous; and, it involves change. Change evokes almost automatic resistance from many in the workplace. Still, most leaders today are expected to be able to lead people into an ambiguous future and inspire them to embrace change. Yes, it is daunting.

It should come as no surprise then that almost all leaders we know have received feedback that they do not have the tools required to enable their people to understand future business requirements, find their place in business plans, or commit to change the level of their contributions. Some leaders have been told that they are "too empathic" and worry too much about "building consensus," while others that they are "not building followership," and are not "hearable" within the organization and its culture. Some have been told that they are "not strategic," and do not know how to "align their teams to a future mission," while others that they are "too strategic" and "cannot turn their ideas into action." What they have in common is that very few understand what their feedback means or how to put it into action to lead people into the future.

When facing the challenge of leading others into the future, the first step is to ensure a strong perspective. Leaders must shift their perspective from "they should follow me because ..." to "I will become the bridge to the future." With that perspective as their lens, the next step is to write themselves a leadership prescription — a plan to achieve their goals.

Our work with leaders over the past decades confirmed a set of leadership tools that those who successfully lead into the future have learned to prescribe and employ effectively. In this section, we share stories about leaders who chose to build those bridges to the future that others were willing to cross:

- Christopher, a motivational sales leader, **Built Committed Followership Through Empathy.**
- Jimmy, a brilliant compensation expert, drove systemic change by **Making the Future Actionable in the Present.**
- Helen, an inspirational executive assistant, taught others the power of **Listening for Possibilities.**
- Sam, a talented and intuitive human resources senior vice president, expanded the thinking of others by **Exploring Innovative Paths to the Future.**

CHAPTER ONE

Build Committed Followership Through Empathy

Organizational hierarchy and rank can dictate compliance. A compliant subordinate does what the manager directs — but not necessarily with any energy or passion. Committed followership is a choice — a choice to do even something different than one would personally choose to do and to steadfastly remain in alignment with a team or a leader's direction. It is more than words. Leaders who embrace the perspective that committed followership is a choice and are willing to invest the time to create a deep commitment to that choice will build the most enduring followership.

The core of the leadership challenge in **Build Committed Followership Through Empathy** is the appreciation of the followership needs of others and the leader's ability to provide for them authentically. We call this **cognitive empathy**.

There are several fundamental capabilities involved in effectively employing this tool:

- Articulate a compelling vision, strategy, and direction.
- Identify essential stakeholders as prospective followers.
- Listen to others' perspectives to understand their commitment needs.
- Make unpopular decisions and lead through contention associated with different perspectives.

COACHING TIPS

DIAL INTO	DIAL-UP	DIAL-DOWN
Your vision, direction, or strategic outcome: Is it clear to potential followers?	• How do you make the vision and direction tangible for potential followers? Are the outcomes clear and measurable? • How will you check for understanding?	• Assumptions about what others should know. • Assumptions about commitment needs of others. • Vague and unclear first steps for each person.
Your business reason for a new vision, direction, or strategic outcome: Is it clear to prospective followers?	Have you clarified for potential followers the **why** behind the future direction you seek?	Assumptions about what others should know.
Commitment needs of prospective followers — what are they looking to see, hear, know, feel from your leadership?	How do you ensure that you understand the commitment needs of your potential followers?	Assumptions about commitment needs of others.
First steps: Are you aligned on the initial steps each follower will take?	Have you ensured that potential followers understand their **first steps** in your vision or a new direction?	Vague and unclear **first steps** for each person.

CHRISTOPHER'S STORY

The Choice to Lead

Christopher's company made the difficult decision to freeze employees retirement benefits and replace them with a more affordable, flexible, and contemporary benefits plan. The Executive Team knew that the field managers were the best-positioned to shepherd their employees through these changes but did not have confidence that, as a group, they would elevate their leadership style to meet the challenge. The changes affected them as well, so they would be more likely to sympathize with the concerns of their employees than to empathize and lead. As expected, the CEO looked to Human Resources to take the lead with all the communication and management of the implementation. Christopher, the Executive Vice President of Global Sales, intervened saying: *This is a big problem for sales, and I believe I know how best to solve it. These changes are going to create contention, confusion, and low productivity among my sales teams. I know what it will take to inform them, support them, and lead them through this. It is our job to get the leaders' hearts in the right place.* Christopher modeled the way, listening actively to their protests and communicating personally with his organization so they could understand the **why** behind these changes. Christopher and his direct reports focused on what the sales force needed most to hear to be comfortable with the changes. They committed to being visible within their organization. They developed action plans to inform and support the sales team, aligned on the first steps they would take together and, ultimately, implemented the program flawlessly. Despite the disruptive changes, the sales team exceeded its revenue and profitability targets for that period.

Leveraging "Hidden Talents"

Christopher chose to become a leader who masterfully built committed followership. Empathy came naturally to him. He quickly and comfortably adjusted his perspective so he could look through the eyes of his potential followers, understand their needs, focus in on those needs, and appeal to the values they shared. He saw and held the perspective of others while balancing their needs with the right decisions for the business — always keeping the business interests as the highest priority. What did not come naturally to Christopher was "contention tolerance," or the willingness to allow and leverage contention while collaborating. He practiced "contention tolerance" and eventually came to appreciate that conflict was a very natural outgrowth of meaningful collaboration and necessary to secure alignment. An abstract thinker by nature, Christopher had to work the hardest at finding his patience with the concrete details that others relied on during times of change. He disciplined himself to help others codify the first steps toward achieving the measurable, targeted contributions that he expected of each of his sales managers. Chris modeled what he expected — excellent leadership that built followership through empathy. Also, he taught his organization to hold up excellence in leadership as the guiding light, and he modeled that in all he did.

It Starts with Perspective

Christopher changed his perspective, designed a prescription that enabled him to find his hidden talents, remedy his problem, and reach new leadership performance heights.

CHRISTOPHER'S PERSPECTIVE SHIFT

> Become a leader who "masterfully" builds committed followership.

Clarify first steps each will take in pursuit of common goals.
Ensure that each understands their first steps and how they fit into the implementation.
Ensure that each is committed, aligned, and actively pursuing their first action steps.

PERFORMANCE

The sales organization exceeded its revenue and profitability targets during the announcement and implementation of benefits changes.

One More Note About Christopher

Christopher chose to become a leader who masterfully built committed followership and prescribed actions that enabled him to achieve that goal. Because of his leadership, the sales force remained productive through the announcement and implementation of these changes. They even exceeded their revenue and profitability targets. Further, Christopher became known across multiple companies for his engaging and inspirational style of developing followership.

OVER AND UNDER-EMPHASIS ON THIS TOOL

When Too Much Emphasis is on Building Committed Followership Through Empathy

Overused empathy can overpower objectivity. When leaders place themselves too comfortably "in the shoes of others" while making decisions of consequence to the business, those decisions tend to be short-sighted. Some resist sharing their real point of view fearing that others will be hurt or will resent their opinions. They may even delay relatively easy decisions in service of seeking stronger consensus. Feedback from their ecosystem, typically suggests that others find them "indecisive," "slow to act," or "conflict-averse."

Does this sound like you or someone you are coaching? You cannot lead if you do not know where you are going. It is difficult to follow someone who does not share a point of view for fear of alienating others. Avoid the role of a neutral third party and practice sharing your point of view after generously listening to the input of others. Find the common threads and help the group surface them. Use those common threads to develop an advanceable solution. Do not let decisions languish.

When Too Little Emphasis is on Building Committed Followership Through Empathy

It is usually imprudent to move to action across the organizational system before ensuring that others are following. Sometimes one can enjoy early, and unencumbered progress toward a goal without the committed followership. However, roadblocks typically spring up along the path in the form of protests or acts of resistance. Empathetic leaders watch the behavior of their followers closely. Are they keeping their commitments? Are they dragging their feet? Are they saying they did not understand what they agreed to do? These are all early signs that the leader did not build adequate followership. Feedback from their ecosystem, typically suggests that these leaders "get tripped up after early progress" and "do not know how to build alignment."

Does this sound like you or someone you are coaching? You are not leading if no one is following you. Acting without followership buy-in will likely lead to resistant behaviors down the road. Consider spending more time building a collective understanding of the plan, expectations for each follower, and expected results before taking too many actions. If you see your followers slowing down or abandoning their commitments, stop, re-convene, pivot if it is called for and re-align.

FINAL TIP

Empathy or Sympathy?

We distinguish **sympathy** as concern for others, a focus on preserving relationships and a desire for harmony within the team or with others across the organization. We distinguish **empathy** as the skill set to create sustainable followership. It requires a deep enough connection with others to understand and provide what they need to see, know, and hear to commit to a common cause. We see more sympathy in the workforce than empathy. It shows up in the form of conflict avoidance, difficulty making tough calls by leaders, and a tendency to preserve relationships at all costs — even costs to business results. Empathic leaders can serve two masters — the business first and their followers as the close second.

The best tip we offer to help you move from sympathy to empathy when faced with a tough decision is to separate it into two distinct questions: *1) **From an objective standpoint, what is best for the business?** And 2) **From a subjective perspective, how can you best deal with the people implications such as retraining, downsizing, firing?***

Acting without followership buy-in will likely lead to resistant behaviors down the road. Consider spending more time building a collective understanding of the plan, expectations for each follower, and anticipated results before taking too many actions. If you see your followers slowing down or abandoning their commitments, stop, re-convene, pivot if it is called for and re-align.

Build Committed Followership Through Empathy
TOOL PRACTICE:

Reflect on the section you have just completed.

1. What is your current perspective?

_____

_____

_____

_____

_____

2. How must you shift your perspective to achieve your goal?

_____

_____

_____

_____

_____

3. What leadership prescriptive actions would you take?

_____

_____

_____

_____

_____

CHAPTER TWO

Making The Future Actionable In The Present

We have found that most of our clients (about 70%) process concrete information easier than they do abstract information. Given the abstract conceptual skills required to envision the future, the leadership challenge in *Making the Future Actionable in the Present* is to translate those abstract ideas into more concrete and tangible actions that others can understand, embrace and apply.

There are several fundamental capabilities involved in effectively employing this tool:

- Understand the longer-term business requirements (18 to the 36-month horizon).
- Explain the future needs of the business in concrete operational terms (i.e., goals, objectives, first steps).
- Understand the prospective followers' level of understanding of the future requirements of the business and where their contributions fit into that future.
- Help prospective followers understand the *first steps* toward embracing future business contributions.

COACHING TIPS

DIAL INTO	DIAL-UP	DIAL-DOWN
Potential followers: What do they need to understand to contribute to the business in the future?	• How have you assessed the commitment needs of your potential followers?	Assumptions about what others *should* know, do know or could find out for themselves.
Potential followers: What must they commit to contributing to the business in the future?	What kinds of information will potential followers need to understand? What contributions will they need to make in the future?	• Templated administrative exercises that are not monitored and re-visited. • Unmonitored plans.
The translation: What is the right balance of concrete versus abstract language required by your potential followers?	How do you tune into the right balance of concrete versus abstract language required by your potential followers?	Too much emphasis on concrete or abstract language.
First steps required from each follower to advance the future agenda.	Clear and measurable targets aligned with future requirements.	Unmonitored targets that do not hold potential followers accountable.

JIMMY'S STORY

The Choice to Lead

Have you ever known a leader who was knowledgeable, brilliant, and usually right but could not seem to get others to follow? That was Jimmy's predecessor, Adam. He was a subject matter expert with an excellent understanding of the business and a natural curiosity for the marketplace, but he did not "suffer fools well;" and, he deemed anyone who did not immediately embrace his ideas about the future as a "fool." Adam extended this sentiment to the CEO's leadership team. When they were slow to embrace his opinions, he dismissed their input and addressed his arguments to the CEO, betting that the CEO would see the brilliance in his work. The CEO sometimes did, but the implementation of Adam's ideas still stalled because the rest of the team was non-supportive at best, typically annoyed by his behavior toward them and others.

Newly promoted to replace Adam, Jimmy had a problem: the department he inherited from Adam did not have the confidence and support of the organization. He had some relationship repair work to do, and he believed that the place to start was by describing his plans in more concrete and actionable terms. Jimmy recognized the importance of aligning the full team by translating future requirements into clear and actionable objectives. He worked with the leadership team to build these objectives, connect them to present actions, and illuminate a clear path to the future. By doing so, Jimmy rebuilt relationships with the leadership team, successfully launched several innovative programs with their full support, and enjoyed a level of success that far exceeded that of his predecessor.

Leveraging "Hidden Talents"

Jimmy was a highly abstract thinker and logical problem-solver. Early in his career, he relied almost exclusively on abstract reasoning to solve problems and on rational persuasion to garner support. Mid-career, Jimmy rotated through a series of large-scale implementation roles. As he practiced his implementation and logistical talents, they became well-honed. Inclined toward abstract analysis and equipped with implementation skills, he turned his attention toward developing his influencing abilities. Jimmy also trained himself to translate abstract and intangible thoughts and reasoning into tangible solutions and to present his ideas in a way that his audience could "hear," understand and find themselves and their part in his solutions. He acquired a peer coach with a strong inclination toward the concrete, and together, they practiced translating his abstract concepts into more tangible actions. He learned to work with others to take their objectives and "engineer backward" at regular intervals. Jimmy taught himself to translate his abstract thoughts into concrete goals, objectives, and actions. With this skill, he was a complete leader who saw many more of his ideas become a reality.

It Starts with Perspective

Jimmy changed his perspective, designed a prescription that enabled him to find his hidden talents, remedy his problem, and reach new leadership performance heights.

JIMMY'S PERSPECTIVE SHIFT

Become a leader who translates abstract ideas into more tangible actions.

> Quiet any pre-conceived notions about what others know or should know regarding the strategic and operational aspects of the business.
>
> Ensure that all potential followers have a good understanding of the future contributions that they can anticipate.
>
> Assess the commitment needs of potential followers and actively engage in meeting them.

PERFORMANCE

> Jimmy re-built relationships with the leadership team, successfully launched several innovative compensation and benefits programs with their full support, and enjoyed the success that far exceeded his predecessor.

One More Note About Jimmy

Jimmy chose to become a leader who communicated and led across strategic and operational dimensions. Because of his leadership, he developed extraordinary credibility across the organization and established a high degree of followership that was required to successfully implement his agenda and advance the business. He was very well regarded throughout the organization for his subject matter expertise and his thought leadership.

OVER AND UNDER-EMPHASIS ON THIS TOOL

When Too Much Emphasis is on Making the Future Actionable in the Present

Some leaders have so much difficulty with abstract reasoning that they slow meetings, or even projects, to a crawl, seeking, presenting, and discussing details with excruciating clarity. They likely prefer to deal with tangible realities than abstract possibilities. They may even show impatience with the reasoning that appears not rooted in facts, data, and logic. Feedback from their ecosystem typically suggests that they "do not deal well with ambiguity," they are "binary," "too concrete" or "not strategic."

> *Does this sound like you or someone you are coaching? If this is you or someone are coaching, consider that you are one of many — and likely in the majority. If you find yourself turning a deaf ear during abstract discussions, try a different course. Ask the presenter to help you understand accurately or in concrete language what they are trying to accomplish and what contributions they need from you. If you are uncomfortable asking in a group setting, write your questions down, and ask later. Likely, you are not the only one in the room struggling to understand.*

When Too Little Emphasis is on Making the Future Actionable in the Present

Some leaders have vast knowledge and valuable ideas but do not seem to be able to advance them to implementation. When asked to explain their ideas in more concrete terms, they become inarticulate and confusing. Their communication can be off-putting for those in the audience and frustrating for the leader because the idea is too powerful to let go but too jumbled to explain. Their listeners may dismiss their views as "random" or "disruptive." Feedback from their ecosystem typically suggests that they are "too lost in their thinking to come down from the clouds and implement."

> *Does this sound like you or someone you are coaching? If you have these moments of unexplainable certainty that you cannot articulate, give yourself space from your argument. Frequently, the logic and reasoning will become explainable with just a little bit of distance. Likely, your intuition is firing faster than you can verbalize. It is OK to share with others that you have not "fully developed your thinking" and commit to sharing*

your thinking with more clarity in the next day or two. Give your cognitive processes time to settle and reveal themselves.

FINAL TIP

"Being Right or Being Heard."

One of the most critical lessons in leadership is that being the smartest person in the room and the most "right" person in the room does not guarantee followership. The shine of the most brilliant visions of the future will dull in the implementation stage if the followers cannot see their role and actions in the execution. The first step in creating followership is to ensure that you can be "heard." Seek to understand what your potential followers need to hear to follow your lead. Listen actively. Practice playing back their words to test understanding. The second step is to adjust your communication style to the needs of the listener. How do you identify their style? Listen carefully and actively to their style and reflect it in your style. The third step is to make sure that you do not make the listener "wrong." When human beings feel "wrong," they shut down, stop listening and start "blamestorming" (or generating ideas about where to place the blame). Finally, be mindful that when trying to be efficient and respond quickly, you may be less clear, and this often leads to misunderstanding. A good practice is to follow up with a call after sending an email on an important topic to ensure that you are understood and heard.

The shine of the most brilliant visions of the future will dull in the implementation stage if the followers cannot see their role and actions in the execution.

Making The Future Actionable In The Present
TOOL PRACTICE:

Reflect on the section you have just completed.

1. What is your current perspective?

_____

_____

_____

_____

_____

2. How must you shift your perspective to achieve your goal?

_____

_____

_____

_____

_____

3. What leadership prescriptive actions would you take?

_____

_____

_____

_____

_____

CHAPTER THREE

Listening For Possibilities

Listening, really listening was always hard — and it's getting harder. In today's world, many things distract people from listening to one another: our thoughts, our mobile devices, others around us, to name a few. We talk about listening in this chapter because the ability to listen is even more critical amid all the distractions everywhere we turn.

There are distractions inside our heads as well — those inner voices that quickly call out what will not work and create resistance to new or innovative ideas. This is why part of active listening is the self-discipline to suspend judgment. How can anyone hear what the other is trying to say when their "inner voices" are screaming disagreement? While it is challenging for leaders to find a way to quiet those inner voices and listen generously, they have the added burden of helping others around them do the same. At the core of the leadership tool, **Listening for Possibilities** is generous listening, with an open mind and heart.

There are several foundational talents and abilities required to use this tool effectively:

- Listen to hear what others are saying and to check your understanding with them.
- Suspend judgment until you fully understand the other person's thinking.
- Enroll others in the possibilities that others offer.

COACHING TIPS

DIAL INTO	DIAL-UP	DIAL-DOWN
Active listening: Is this a talent for you?	What actions can you take to ensure that you are actively listening?	• Distractions. • Assumptions about others' motives. • Pre-conceived ideas about what others will say.
Participative understanding: Are you willing to "own" your accountability as a listener?	How can you test for understanding? Are you restating what you believe the other has said? Are you asking questions?	Assumptions about what you believe you are hearing.
Suspending judgment: Will you listen through the automatic voices of adverse judgment?	• How can you best avoid early judgments about innovative ideas? • Are you listening to the person or the idea?	• Turn off the immediate and "automatic voices" of judgment. • Perceived "road-blocks" that you have imagined.
Enrolling others in the possibilities you hear.	What actions can you take to build followership for innovative ideas?	Any tendency to abdicate your leadership to others.

HELEN'S STORY

The Choice to Lead

The market environment requires speed, adaptability, and cross-organizational collaboration — all of which underscore the imperative for all in the organization, regardless of role, seniority, or specific scope of responsibilities to listen for possibilities. Helen modeled this form of leadership. She was an executive assistant who became one of the most inspirational leaders of change we have ever known. She was a quiet, reserved woman and a very humble employee who was so grateful for our business and the people in it that she embraced every need and request for change (i.e., to reduce cost, to promote quality) with her whole mind and heart. The uniqueness of Helen was that she listened generously for the possibilities in each initiative and pursued them while most of the team just resisted them and treated them as the next "flavor of the month." Helen was able to quiet all voices of judgment, including her own, and listen generously for the value of each request.

When the corporation launched a request to "take work out of the system," Helen saw some possible areas to explore but was unsure of her ability to generate support. Helen's problem: how could she create followership to "listen for the possibility" inherent in some of her ideas and initiatives? She found multiple opportunities with ease — the challenge was to develop the followership among her peers to successfully implement them. She engaged the right people, clearly articulated the required changes and the reasons for these changes. Helen had access to C-Suite officers and vice presidents that she never used — instead, she worked the issues with colleagues on the teams potentially affected by her plan. In the end, she was successful at winning full system support for her ideas, achieving the cost and productivity savings. She became a significant contributor to all productivity efforts of the business and made a tremendous difference — her efforts would yield significant cost savings and exponentially more in productivity.

Leveraging "Hidden Talents"

Helen had many extraordinary gifts as a leader. Specifically, as a productivity leader, she was naturally inclined to seek and find root causes with high precision, willing to challenge the status quo and open to listening for possibilities in new and innovative ideas. She was not naturally inclined to enroll others in creative ideas, nor was she inclined to engage in the contention that is sometimes required to break down roadblocks along the path. She embraced these as her leadership goals and practiced translating possibilities into concrete plans that others could see and action. She anticipated contention but committed herself to lead through it to create an aligned commitment to these new ideas. Slowly but surely, her practice resulted in solid leadership skills.

It Starts with Perspective

Helen changed her perspective, designed a prescription that enabled her to find her hidden talents, remedy her problem, and reach new leadership performance heights.

HELEN'S PERSPECTIVE SHIFT

> Become a colleague who listens generously to others and helps others do the same.

LEADERSHIP PRESCRIPTION

> Continue listening for possibilities by quieting the "inner voices" of resistance.

> Translate the possibilities into concrete actions for self and others.

> Tolerate contention and resistance and help people see the possibilities as she sees them.

> She was successful at winning full system support for her plans, achieving the cost and productivity savings.

One More Note About Helen

Mother Teresa once said, "there are no great deeds, just small ones done with great love." Helen chose to become the embodiment of that quote in our company — by becoming a colleague who listened generously to others and leading from where she was. She became a significant contributor to all productivity efforts of the business and made a tremendous difference. Because of all the times she "listened generously" to others, the business and the team were enormously enriched.

OVER AND UNDER-EMPHASIS ON THIS TOOL

When Too Much Emphasis is on Listening for Possibilities

Some leaders tend to over-nurture ideas, perspectives, and even other people's performance issues to the exclusion of making decisions and taking actions that advance the business. For example, they can become so committed to seeing what is possible for another, that they may avoid taking action on their current, poor performance. Feedback from their ecosystem suggests that these leaders are slow to decide, too patient with poor performers and processes, and, generally, indecisive.

> ***Does this sound like you or someone you are coaching?*** *Do you, or others, you lead put too much emphasis on seeing the possibilities for ideas, perspectives, and even people to the exclusion of making and advancing decisions. Instead, ensure that you or the people you lead have measurable objectives and that expectations are timebound. If the results do not materialize, evaluate the prudence of continuing your investment.*

When Too Little Emphasis is on Listening for Possibilities

Some leaders tend to shut down possible ideas, perspectives, and creative solutions before enough consideration and exploration. They may be quite happy to rely on people, processes, and cultural traditions that maintain the status quo that has enabled their success thus far. Feedback from their ecosystem suggests that these leaders are "caught in business as usual."

Does this sound like you or someone you are coaching? Consider that you may be reacting too quickly based on a prior experience that seems to match the current situation. Become an active listener by suspending your judgments and seeking to appreciate the different perspectives of others. Test your understanding by asking questions and repeating what you believe you heard. Turn down the volume on your "no" and up the volume on your "maybe;" and, turn down the volume of your "but" and up the volume of your "and."

FINAL TIP

Choosing to "Lead from Where You Are."

The concept of "leading from where you are," meaning that every employee provides and influences the best possible performance that the organization can achieve, has been around for years and it is still one of the best routes to increased productivity. For this reason, forward-thinking organizations are increasingly looking for people at every level to lead others to better performance and productivity. When you see emerging leaders within your organization who are willing to think innovatively about their work and set achievable targets for new levels of performance and productivity, we encourage you to support their efforts. Where appropriate, enable their efforts by helping to remove roadblocks and celebrate their successes. These emerging leaders will bring a passion for innovative thinking and implementation that will be inspirational throughout the organization.

Become an active listener by suspending your judgments and seeking to appreciate the different perspectives of others. Test your understanding by asking questions and repeating what you believe you heard.

Listening For Possibilities TOOL PRACTICE:

Reflect on the section you have just completed.

1. What is your current perspective?

_____

_____

_____

_____

_____

2. How must you shift your perspective to achieve your goal?

_____

_____

_____

_____

_____

3. What leadership prescriptive actions would you take?

_____

_____

_____

_____

_____

CHAPTER FOUR

Exploring Innovative Paths To The Future

Some leaders are inclined to take things at face value. They focus on what they see or touch. Other leaders perceive the world through their mind's eye — discerning what is not physically present but present in the world of ideas and intuition. These leaders are more intuitive and abstract in their thinking. Rather than noticing three separate events, such as three employees struggling with a new process and addressing each separately, they will look for and find patterns to their difficulties and address them. The patterns and trends they notice lead them to predict future conditions in their workplace or market. These leaders must be careful to scrutinize the patterns they choose to use predictively and ensure their relevance to the priorities at hand, or they might find themselves unfocused and lost in their world of ideas.

At the core of the leadership tool, **Exploring Innovative Paths to the Future**, are three different challenges — to connect the dots, to connect the right dots, and to help others see paths to the future.

There are several foundational talents and abilities required to use this tool effectively:

- Search for and recognize patterns and trends.
- Filter out those patterns and trends that are not relevant to the business requirements.
- Help others to recognize the right patterns and trends.
- Use patterns and trends to enroll followers in aligned future actions.

COACHING TIPS

DIAL INTO	DIAL-UP	DIAL-DOWN
Patterns and trends: How talented are you at recognizing them?	• Your talent for performing root cause analysis. • The *why* question to probe beyond face value?	The tendency to react to isolated, uninterpreted datapoints.
Patterns and trends: How disciplined are you at distinguishing and prioritizing business consistent with patterns and trends?	Your discipline to prioritize the patterns and trends that are consistent with the business requirements so that you do not lose followers by investing in "start and stop initiatives."	A tendency to see patterns and trends as a result, instead of a means to an outcome.
Patterns and trends that help you and your followers explore the first concrete steps toward the future.	Ask: Where do these patterns and trends lead me? Do they point to some tangible future direction or outcome?	Vague action steps and time commitments.
How do you enroll and align your followers in a future direction?	• Illuminate the future vision. • Clarify the concrete first steps required of your followers.	Day-to-day distractions that divert attention from the future imperatives of the business.

SAM'S STORY

The Choice to Lead

There is data, and there is information. Many leaders do not stop to notice the significant difference between the two. Sam recognized the difference, so when his company decided to focus on responding quickly to the results of the Employee Commitment Survey, he saw the danger. Sam was afraid that his colleagues would react too swiftly and create action plans from the data alone. He became the first to offer an alternative. Sam encouraged his colleagues to take the results of the survey into their client groups and conduct focus groups so that they could understand what the survey results suggested. He became, the leader of the ad hoc team that led the analysis of that, was formed to analyze the focus group input and, together, they identified key patterns and trends. They then compared the trend data to future priorities of the business, careful not to follow any irrelevant paths. Finally, they made real connections between the trends and patterns they identified to the future imperatives of the business. They connected the dots between the present and the future and built plans to increase employee commitment now and into the future. Those plans resulted in sustained and significant increases in employee commitment results. By recognizing trends and patterns, Sam translated them into current actions, and he was able to create innovative paths to the future that not only solved for the employee commitment issues but were relevant to the future business needs.

Leveraging "Hidden Talents"

Sam was a highly intelligent leader who had lightning-quick intuition. He was creative and had a natural ability to see patterns and trends and make connections. What did not come naturally to him was the ability to quiet all of the ideas and options that Sam associated with those patterns and trends.

However, he learned to turn down the volume on his "idea channel" when the patterns that came into his mind's eye did not connect well to the future business requirements. He also helped others learn to find patterns by coaching them to keep lists of recurring issues and ask **why** until the root cause was determined. He recognized when the information was insufficient or irrelevant, and he trained himself to step away from it and not follow its path. While his intuition and ability to see those patterns and trends came naturally to him, his ability to translate that into structured implementation plans was a challenge. He occasionally over-estimated the capacity of the organization to deliver. So, he supplemented his leadership talents by hiring implementation specialists who could help him bring his ideas to reality. Working with those specialists, he sharpened his "implementation talents" and learned to bring them forward in similar instances. He trained himself to be a complete leader in this area of exploring innovative paths that connected to the future.

It Starts with Perspective

Sam changed his perspective, designed a prescription that enabled him to find his hidden talents, remedy his problem, and reach new leadership performance heights.

SAM'S PERSPECTIVE SHIFT

> Become a leader who builds paths between now and the future.

LEADERSHIP PRESCRIPTION

> Quiet the inclination to follow all the paths that patterns and trends suggest while helping others to see relevant patterns and trends.

> Ensure sufficient prioritization of patterns and trends by relevance to the business to avoid "start and stop" initiatives.

> Clarify in concrete terms how patterns and trends connect to future business needs.

PERFORMANCE

> By ensuring that the team focused on the patterns and trends that were relevant to the employee commitment survey and the business priorities, the team created action plans that resulted in significantly higher levels of employee commitments.

One More Note About Sam

Sam chose to become a leader who built paths between the present and the future and ensured that people followed those paths. He became highly valued for his superior analytical skills, strategic thinking, and ability to illuminate pathways for his followers between the present and the future. Sam successfully trained himself and others to stop many ill-conceived initiatives before they started and launched many that positively impacted the business. He went on to apply his analytical and strategic ability to enrich several different corporate cultures.

OVER AND UNDER-EMPHASIS ON THIS TOOL

When Too Much Emphasis is on Exploring Innovative Paths to the Future

Some leaders are more interested in generating ideas and options than they are in determining which course to take. They may lack discipline and focus, and chase each new idea that comes to them — creating a list of incomplete projects or initiatives. They may read into things or over-interpret things and may even draw erroneous conclusions. Implementations may slip under their leadership. Feedback from their ecosystem typically suggests that these leaders are "not focused" and "all over the place."

> *Does this sound like you or someone you are coaching?* *Try to keep lists of innovative ideas and possibilities. Note those that reoccur over time and suggest a pattern or trend. Discipline yourself to focus and to ensure that these ideas are relevant and aligned to the business agenda. Collaborate with a colleague who is talented at implementation. Determine together which ideas have the best chance of successful implementation and solve issues of critical importance to the business.*

When Too Little Emphasis is on Exploring Innovative Paths to the Future

Some leaders take things more literally. They accept things at face value and will be less likely to seek root causes, to see patterns and connections, or to interpret what is available "beyond their five senses." They prefer to focus on tangible realities and prefer the practical over the abstract. Feedback from their ecosystem typically suggests that these leaders are "too concrete," "too literal," "miss the big picture," and are "not strategic."

> *Does this sound like you or someone you are coaching?* *Focus more of your attention on identifying trends and patterns that surface in your business and listen for possibilities, even though abstract. It is hard to have a vision for the development of a company or its leaders if you cannot see and believe in what could be possible. Consider keeping lists of reoccurring issues and successes that may inform patterns, trends, or possibilities. Practice asking **why** and probing for root causes. Ask a trusted colleague who is more inclined toward abstract thinking to look at the reoccurrences with you to find patterns and root causes.*

FINAL TIP

"Option" or "Possibility"

We distinguish a ***possibility*** as something that could become an ***option*** and an option as something that is under consideration for selection. We notice a strong tendency for leaders to move quickly to discuss options without taking the time to consider possibilities. The options that we quickly generate, we frequently recall from our experience rather than from the world of possibilities and innovative thinking. Thus, those options are likely to produce "business as usual decisions." We encourage leaders to be more "possibility curious" to invest more energy in generating innovative ideas and to practice seeing possibilities that will lead them to find creative solutions. Next time you think about disagreeing with someone else's thinking, consider distinguishing the ***possibility*** of it from the ***option*** of it. You may create an opening for an innovative approach that would have otherwise been shut down before being adequately vetted. You will serve yourself and the organization well to allow some exploration of possible paths to the future — even the ones that sound crazy.

We encourage leaders to be more "possibility curious" to invest more energy in generating innovative ideas and to practice seeing possibilities that will lead them to find creative solutions. Next time you think about disagreeing with someone else's thinking, consider distinguishing the *possibility* of it from the *option* of it.

Exploring Innovative Paths To The Future
TOOL PRACTICE:

Reflect on the section you have just completed.

1. What is your current perspective?

_____

_____

_____

_____

_____

2. How must you shift your perspective to achieve your goal?

_____

_____

_____

_____

_____

3. What leadership prescriptive actions would you take?

_____

_____

_____

_____

_____

PART TWO:
TOOLS FOR BUILDING CONNECTIONS THAT ADVANCE THE BUSINESS

"All are connected ... no one thing can change by itself."

PAUL HAWKEN

One of the most powerful networks in the workplace is the informal network of people connections. Some of us are better networkers than others, but few of us learn to use the full power of relationships to advance the interests of the business and its stakeholders. Many of the leaders we know are challenged to develop more balanced connections. Some hear that they "over-use" their connections in certain areas of the business, while others hear that they "under-use" their connections. Some hear that they become the connection rather than ensuring that the right individuals are connected. Others hear that they do not "adapt their style of communication to their audience." The majority receive feedback that they do not leverage different ways of thinking because they do not creatively connect and collaborate with others.

When facing the challenge of building connections that advance the business, the first step is to ensure a sufficiently broad perspective. Leaders must first shift their perspective from "connections are a nice to have" to "connections are a must to build and leverage" to advance the business. Success in today's workplace requires that leaders expand from their silos or their team and collaborate across organizational boundaries. With this perspective as their new lens, the next step is to write themselves a prescription — a plan to achieve their leadership goal.

Our work with leaders over the past decades confirmed a set of leadership tools that those who successfully built connections that advanced the business learned to prescribe and employ effectively. In this section, we share stories about leaders who chose to secure relationships across the organization and, by doing so, strengthened the business.

- Michael, a hands-on, operational CFO, who provided balanced leadership by **Enabling Strategic Focus Through Supportive Connections.**
- Melissa, a highly intuitive general manager, who provided powerful leadership through ambiguity, by **Leading Through "White Space Connections.**
- Matt, a business-process expert who achieved exceptional results, demonstrated the importance of **Adapting Your Style to Meaningfully Connect.**
- Suzie, an extraordinary diversity officer who drove inclusion by teaching others to **Explore Differences Through Creative Connections.**

CHAPTER FIVE

Enabling Strategic Focus Through Supportive Connections

Some leaders have a natural tendency toward the longer-term, strategic aspects of the business while others tend to gravitate toward the shorter-term and operational aspects of the business. The challenge for all leaders is to find an effective way to lead across all aspects of the strategic — operational continuum. For some, this means that they must become more disciplined about prioritization and commit to allocating the time to focus on their less favored side of the continuum. For others, this means that they supplement their talents by hiring capabilities which complement them and help them draw out their own "hidden talents."

At the core of the leadership tool, **Enabling Strategic Focus Through Supportive Connections** is developing a good understanding of the entire business and the resourcefulness to leverage connections that enable an appropriate balance of both strategic and operational leadership.

There are several foundational talents and abilities required to use this tool effectively:

- Understand the long and short-term requirements and priorities of the business.
- Understand the informal organization as a system of connections and how to leverage them.
- Understand and leverage a more formal governance system of connections and how to leverage them.

COACHING TIPS

DIAL INTO	DIAL-UP	DIAL-DOWN
Long and short-term requirements of the business: Ensure that you have a working understanding of both.	Actions that will enable a better working understanding of any gaps in your knowledge of the business requirements.	Any tendency to over-emphasize or under-emphasize the long-term or the short-term.
The informal organization as a system: Who does what and how are the connections leveraged?	The actions you can take to strengthen your informal connections across the business.	• The tendency to connect only when necessary. • The tendency to build connections only within your immediate area.
The formal business governance practices: How are the connections across the business ensured?	Hold others accountable through business objectives.	• The tendency to hold others accountable through hierarchy or rank.

MICHAEL'S STORY

The Choice to Lead

Michael was a capable and experienced general manager with broad financial skills. This expertise suited him well for a Chief Financial Officer role in a sizeable spin-off business that was challenged to solve two simultaneous variables: 1) reduce high cost in almost all areas of the company, and 2) grow the bottom line through new markets and product introductions. Michael's talents tended toward the operations side of the business, and his favorite strategy was driving efficiencies, so the organization he designed reflected these preferences. However, he faced a problem when the presidents of the business segments complained to the CEO that the finance organization was not adequately supporting the plans to grow their businesses — instead they were all focused on the details of day-to-day business operations. Michael decided to split his organization holding the "control" functions of finance close and dispatching small teams of well-trained financial analysts and planners, who were focused more on the strategic priorities, into the businesses to report jointly to the presidents and himself. He made sure that the "finance business partners," as they were titled, would involve him in their long-term planning and business decisions.

Additionally, he ensured that he spent time with all members of his team, leveraging both their operational and strategic knowledge, which allowed him to build new skills for himself. Michael never became entirely comfortable relying on others for his information, but, over time, he became more willing to count on others for support. He solved the balance of strategic and operational by developing and leveraging connections among business segments and corporate functions.

Leveraging "Hidden Talents"

Michael was born to run things, control resources, and deal in concrete facts and plans. Operational details gave him great comfort, and he often used them as a sharp influencing tool, sometimes even embarrassing colleagues with them and earning the dubious title "master of the gotcha." Armed with "the answers," he saw collaboration as a burden. Over time, he learned that eventually, his progress would stall if he had not secured stakeholder support. As he ascended to senior ranks, he was expected to balance the operational details and the future priorities of the business. Given a choice, he would have suggested: "just let me run everything, and I will make it work."

The first step in Michael's development was to change that perspective from "let me control everything" to "how do I strengthen my connections and learn to influence what I do not control?" He supplemented his natural talents by hiring those with different skills and experience than himself. He expanded his oversight by delegating effectively, and he frequently prioritized with senior management to develop an understanding of what details were important to them. He even negotiated with senior management to include key leaders within his organization in discussions at the appropriate times, acknowledging that he did not have all the details top of mind. He began to make a list of crucial stakeholder connections, engaged them in the planning, followed up with them regularly, reset plans if problems arose, and ensured that he and everyone kept their commitments. None of this came naturally to Michael, but he chose to practice building supporting connections with his stakeholders. These connections enabled him to stay at an appropriate strategic level and lead the analysis of future marketplace trends and plans without compromising his oversight of the operation, thus balancing the strategic and the operational.

It Starts with Perspective

Michael changed his perspective, designed a prescription that enabled him to find his hidden talents, remedy his problem, and reach new leadership performance heights.

MICHAEL'S PERSPECTIVE SHIFT

> Become a leader who artfully balances the strategic and operational through supportive stakeholder connections.

LEADERSHIP PRESCRIPTION

> Quiet my inclination to connect with others only "as needed."

> Engage the informal organizational system of connections outside of my silo that is required to perform effectively and efficiently.

> Determine the most significant actions to take to build and leverage both informal and formal connections.

PERFORMANCE

> Michael developed an organization that effectively surfaced and addressed both the strategic and operational challenges of the business by leveraging connections — and solved for "two simultaneous variables."

One More Note about Michael

Michael chose to become a leader who artfully balanced the strategic and operational through supportive stakeholder connections. He was able to solve for both the strategic and the operational by leveraging others across his new organization.

OVER AND UNDER-EMPHASIS ON THIS TOOL

When Too Much Emphasis is on Enabling a Strategic Focus Through Supportive Connections

Some leaders are more inclined to focus on the strategic priorities of the business and marketplace and tend to leave the operations and its oversight to others. They prefer to spend their time on longer-term strategic priorities. Feedback from their ecosystem typically suggests that these leaders are "operating at too high a level and are not finding the right opportunities to intervene with early detection and resolution of issues within their operations." More often than not, the right interventions would become more apparent with the right connections in place and fully leveraged.

> *Does this sound like you or someone you are coaching? Experiment with ways to balance your attention and depth of knowledge. If you have capable and skilled operations leaders on your team, we encourage you to use their skills but to remain connected to the oversight. Conduct regular operations reviews to keep yourself current in the operations of your business and to keep you alert to areas that might require more focused attention. If you are not a detail person, it is best to keep the details close at hand.*

When Too Little Emphasis is on Enabling a Strategic Focus Through Supportive Connections

Many leaders believe that they are forced to stay in the details because they are expected to be able to produce detailed information or to answer all questions in detail. At the same time, they are asked to be "more strategic." In some cases, these individuals are not inclined to lift their thinking above the details. In other cases, they may have the preference but lack the time. Feedback from their ecosystem typically suggests that these leaders are too far "in the weeds" or too focused on the details.

***Does this sound like you or someone you are coaching?** Find ways to network and connect with those external to your business — what is happening and what is likely to happen with customers, markets, products, services, and leaders. Consider delegating competitive, external market analysis to a member of your team and delegating more of the operations and detail management to someone else. You do not have to "be the balance." Your role is to "provide balanced leadership." In other words, you do not have to do all the work that provides the balance, but you do have to make sure you achieve the balance.*

FINAL TIP

Developing or Supplementing Personal Leadership

Through the years, we heard fewer phrases spoken to us more frequently by leaders than "I'm too old to change." Although that is not a leadership prescription we support, sometimes this belief is so deeply embedded in their thinking that we start by working around it. Sometimes we begin our discussions with how to supplement their skills to enhance their leadership performance. For Michael, the first steps were to help him develop the confidence to let go of control and to help him build a plan that enabled him to surround himself with the capability he needed to excel so that he could assume a position of balanced oversight of the strategic and the operational. Once he became comfortable that all the issues were in competent hands and the details were just a phone call away, it was easier to help him practice more focused attention on the strategic priorities of his business. Ultimately, he did change his style and developed into a more inclusive and balanced leader.

You do not have to "be the balance."
Your role is to "provide balanced
leadership." In other words, you
do not have to do all the work that
provides the balance, but you do
have to make sure you achieve
the balance.

Enabling A Strategic Focus Through Supportive Connections TOOL PRACTICE:

Reflect on the section you have just completed.

1. What is your current perspective?

_____

_____

_____

_____

_____

2. How must you shift your perspective to achieve your goal?

_____

_____

_____

_____

_____

3. What leadership prescriptive actions would you take?

_____

_____

_____

_____

_____

CHAPTER SIX

Leading Through "White Space" Connections

As businesses become more global and complex, the workplace continues to grow more challenged by issues that emerge and have no clear owner (the "white spaces" that fall between the boxes on the organizational chart and are not formally assigned). Leaders who have a good sense of how work and processes flow across the organization are in an advantageous position to anticipate these "white space" outages or disconnects — and make the connections that remedy them.

At the core of the leadership tool, **Leading Through Whitespace Connections** is a good sense of the workflow patterns across the organization and those individuals best suited to address any issues that emerge.

There are several foundational talents and abilities required to use this tool effectively:

- Predict and detect breakdowns and disconnects in process or functions across the business.
- Connect the right parts of the system to resolve "white space" disruptions or disconnects.
- Hold the right people accountable.

COACHING TIPS

DIAL INTO	DIAL-UP	DIAL-DOWN
Organizational Awareness: Do you have a good sense of the organization and its workflow patterns?	Your level of awareness of organizational workflow patterns, processes, and connections across the business.	Focus within your organization or silo.
Diagnostic talents: Do you have a suitable means of quickly detecting breakdowns in connections or process?	How you detect early signs that breakdowns are emerging in the system.	A tendency to wait for outages before you respond.
Cross-organizational accountabilities: Do you understand the responsibilities of others across different organizations?	The actions you can take to strengthen connections to individuals accountable for these outages.	The tendency to fix the outage yourself.
How do you best hold others across the system accountable?	How you maintain the connections and oversight of the solution.	The assumption that assigning it means it will happen as assigned.

MELISSA'S STORY

The Choice to Lead

While many of her colleagues were vying for power during a reorganization, Melissa distanced herself from the organizational dynamics and paid attention to the functioning of the organization. The ambiguity of the organizational change caused many outages — especially in the connections between leaders, their organizations, and their regulatory processes. While her colleagues focused on their "box" on the new organization chart, Melissa concentrated on the "white space" between the assigned "boxes" on the organization chart where the blockages and outages in workflow were occurring. She anticipated the issues or saw them quickly, called for the right teams of leaders to intervene, provided oversight, and went back to her regular accountabilities until the next outage occurred. When the time came to fill in the "boxes" on the organizational chart, Melissa was overseeing so many of the vulnerable "white space" areas already that her role was enlarged to include them.

Leveraging "Hidden Talents"

While it is tempting to ignore the "white spaces" as "not my problem," we find them to be "Petri dishes" where destructive organizational breakdowns, unspecified connections, and undesignated or unclear accountabilities breed. Few leaders are as naturally inclined to operate inside of the ambiguous "white space" as Melissa. She saw things fall into these "white spaces" and was drawn to jump in and fix them. However, as she grew in seniority and experience, so did the breadth of her role. She could no longer be the "fixer" of all things — despite her powerful inclination to do so. She saw that she needed to change her preference from "see it and fix it" to "see it and connect the right people to solve it." She disciplined herself to make the right connections to address issues without fixing them herself.

Her colleagues described her style as the "seagull approach" — fly above with oversight, dive down to make connections, and return quickly to the higher levels of monitoring. It was in that manner that she led through and leveraged the right connections to remedy the "white space" outages.

It Starts with Perspective

Melissa changed her perspective, designed a prescription that enabled her to find her hidden talents, remedy her problem, and reach new leadership performance heights.

MELISSA'S PERSPECTIVE SHIFT

> Become a leader who leverages the right connections to lead through "white space" outages.

LEADERSHIP PRESCRIPTION

> Quiet my inclination to fix things by myself.

> Ensure a good understanding of the workflow and accountabilities of others in the organization.

> Continually look for opportunities to strengthen proactive connections across the organization.

PERFORMANCE

> By demonstrating an ability to leverage connections while providing adequate oversight, Melissa advanced her organization and the broader business organization.

One More Word About Melissa

Melissa chose to become a leader who connected the disconnects across the organizational "white spaces." Because of her outstanding ability to lead through ambiguity and her keen sense of accountability for the organization, she came as close as we have seen to perfecting the art of leading large functional organizations that directly contributed to the advancement of the business.

OVER AND UNDER-EMPHASIS ON THIS TOOL

When "White Space Connections" are Over-Emphasized

Some leaders are responsibility magnets. They are team players who cannot stand to see work languishing. Work seems to gravitate to them, so they jump in and take it on. They anticipate gaps in responsibilities, intervene to resolve them and return to their accountabilities. Occasionally, others may even take advantage of their sense of responsibility, leaving them and their team overburdened and feeling resentful or even behind in their assigned duties. Feedback from their ecosystem frequently suggests that these leaders are "playing out of position" or "in the weeds" too often.

> *Does this sound like you or someone you are coaching?*
> *Do not allow your tendencies to put yourself or your team into jeopardy because of your impulse to dive in and fix everything. It is all right to facilitate or even lead an intervention designed to avoid organizational outages, but it is best to connect the right leaders to fix the problem and then either provide oversight or back away. Leaders who become the "doers" of all the things can create unintended collateral damage such as distracting, overburdening or even demotivating their team or themselves.*

When "White Space Connections" are Under-Emphasized

Some leaders are responsibility deflectors. They have the frustrating tendency to point out work that has yet to be done by others but rarely volunteer themselves to help others, and certainly, do not take on any extra work themselves. They do not step into the "white spaces." The work they deflect can fall on others and often leads to resentment. Feedback from their ecosystem typically suggests that these leaders are "not good team players."

> ***Does this sound like you or someone you are coaching?*** *Be careful about the story that could be developing about you among your team, colleagues, and management. Are you becoming known as "the Teflon," team member (the person to whom no work sticks)? We encourage you to reflect upon your level of commitment to the team, organization, and business. We also suggest that you seek feedback from those in your ecosystem regarding your style. Your intent may be to challenge unnecessary work or unclear accountabilities, but your impact may be different than you desire.*

FINAL TIP

"The Seagull Approach"

You may have been given feedback to flex more of your strategic muscles and pull yourself up from the tactics. We often see quite a bit of frustration in leaders who receive this feedback. The disappointment is rooted in the belief that the leaders who are giving this feedback are the ones who continually put tactical work into the system that distracts leaders from their strategic imperatives. In these cases, we always suggest "The Seagull Approach." Notice your relationship to issues as they arise. Are you quick to spot them, or are you on the slow side? Do you dive in and fix them yourself? Take the **who** out of the equation. **What** needs to happen? Someone needs to notice the outages quickly, and someone needs to fix them, right? If you are slow to see, partner with someone quick to understand issues and learn the early warning signs. If you are inclined to fix things, practice making the connections with the right people who can fix them and hold them accountable.

If you are inclined to fix things, practice making the connections with the right people who can fix them and hold them accountable.

Leading Through "White Space" Connections
TOOL PRACTICE:

Reflect on the section you have just completed.

1. What is your current perspective?

_____

_____

_____

_____

_____

2. How must you shift your perspective to achieve your goal?

_____

_____

_____

_____

_____

3. What leadership prescriptive actions would you take?

_____

_____

_____

_____

_____

CHAPTER SEVEN

Adapt Your Style To Meaningfully Connect

In today's workplace, leaders cannot only rely on their rank, title, and place in the hierarchy (vertically) to direct others. Successful leaders learn to adapt their style to influence people across the organization (horizontally) to collectively advance the business.

We have found that the most effective way to understand how to best influence someone is to observe how they influence others. Leaders who recognize this and adapt their style to meet the influencing needs of others develop the most powerful influencing skills and committed followership. While this seems simple as an influencing strategy, it is not as simple as it looks because so much of communication and influencing style is automatic.

At the core of **Adapting Your Style to Meaningfully Connect** is the ability to identify key stakeholders and adapt to their influencing requirements.

There are several foundational talents and abilities required to use this tool effectively:

- Identify essential partners you need to connect with and influence.
- Recognize different and preferred influencing styles.
- Ensure meaningful connections by adapting your influencing style.

COACHING TIPS

DIAL INTO	DIAL-UP	DIAL-DOWN
Stakeholder Connections: How do you identify and build connections with the key stakeholders.	Your understanding of the formal and informal leaders in the organization who you must influence to advance the business.	The tendency to only focus on established relationships.
Knowledge of influencing styles: Do you understand the influencing techniques well enough to recognize distinctive styles in others.	Actions can you take to develop a deeper understanding of different influencing styles.	The tendency to rely more on control and hierarchy to influence.
Shifting styles: Are you willing to adapt your style to build more meaningful connections?	Opportunities to adapt your style to influence others with different styles.	• Assumptions about what influences others. • The belief that shifting your style will not make a difference.

MATTHEW'S STORY

The Choice to Lead

Matthew was responsible for setting up a state-of-the-art Employee Service Center in his company. He was skilled at creating complex processes enabled by technology, which seemed to suit him perfectly for the role. The problem was the employees did not want to use the new Service Center. They continued to go to their human resources department for their administrative needs, and about half of the human resources department was happy to stay in that capacity. The other half of the human resources department was pleased with the new arrangements and continued to refer all employee inquiries to the Service Center. Matthew recognized that the desire to provide superior customer service was a powerful motivator for the Service Center Employees, so he worked with them to develop plans to ensure an excellent customer experience for each employee who called the Service Center. When the formal communication programs failed to bring employees to the Service Center, he and his team went on the road to reach out personally and influence the employees to trust the Service Center with their needs. Matthew also connected with the human resources employees individually to change their thinking about the Service Center. He recognized that the group of human resources employees who did not want to give up their administrative roles feared that the Service Center would take over their work and place their jobs in jeopardy. Many of the human resources employees were better suited to work in the Service Center, so Matthew arranged for their transfers. In approaching the other group of human resources employees who wanted to drop their administrative duties immediately, he negotiated a transition period. Within six months, the Employee Service Center was exceeding their targeted rates of service. By adapting his influencing style, with both the employees and the human resources department, he built meaningful connections with each of these constituents and advanced the progress of the Service Center.

Leveraging "Hidden Talents"

For Matthew, the skills associated with adapting his influencing style did not come naturally or easily. Matthew was naturally caring and wanted to help others, but he came to understand that people needed more than his warm heart and helping hand to change established work habits and embrace new processes. Early on, Matthew was inclined to leverage formal communication channels (official, vertical channels). Through years of development, he learned to reach out informally, personally and directly — across the organization (horizontal) — to enlist the support and commitment required for successful implementation. Matthew also discovered that one style of influence did not work across all situations or even sub-groups of people. So, he dialed into his natural sensitivity, practiced recognizing the influencing needs of others, and adapted his style to ensure the meaningful connections that helped to advance the business.

It Starts with Perspective

Matthew changed his perspective, designed a prescription that enabled him to find his hidden talents, remedy his problem, and reach new leadership performance heights.

MATTHEW'S PERSPECTIVE SHIFT

Become a leader who builds meaningful connections by adapting influencing style to ensure business progress.

LEADERSHIP PRESCRIPTION

Quiet assumptions about what it takes to influence others.
Study the styles of influence used by crucial partners as useful indicators of how they are most effectively influenced.
Adapt style to meet their influencing needs.

> Matthew established the Employee Service Center as a remarkable success and model for the industry.

One More Note About Matthew

Matthew chose to become a leader who ensured meaningful connections to advance business progress. By recognizing the influencing needs of each group and adapting his influencing style to connect in a meaningful way, Matthew established the Employee Service Center as a remarkable success and model for the industry.

OVER AND UNDER-EMPHASIS ON THIS TOOL

When Too Much Emphasis is on Adapting Your Style to Meaningfully Connect

Some leaders are chameleon-like in their style, almost "becoming" the person or group they attempt to influence. That is not the intention of this leadership tool. These individuals prioritize form over the purpose and can appear as "political" and inauthentic. Feedback from their ecosystem often suggests that these leaders seem to have their "own agenda."

> *Does this sound like you or someone you are coaching?*
> *In today's workplace, leaders must learn to deal effectively with both style and substance. Watch for the body language, the facial expressions, the off-point questions, and the silence, all of which are good indicators that employees or even colleagues need more targeted substance to your message to meaningfully connect and be open to your influence. If you notice these signs, pause to make sure that you are connecting in the manner you intend. Most important, don't lose sight of the purpose — which is to meaningfully connect and influence as a means of advancing the business, not promoting yourself.*

When Too Little Emphasis is on Adapting Your Style to Meaningfully Connect

A leader's automatic influencing style will not always connect with or influence others. Over-dependence on one personal form of influence will likely stall any leader at some point in their career. Feedback from their ecosystem typically suggests that these leaders are "rigid" or are "not engaging" or are "uniform in their influencing approach."

> *Does this sound like you or someone you are coaching? We encourage you to re-frame your thinking and try this. Be patient, listen, and watch for different clues that others will give you about how they influence others. Likely, that style will work to influence them as well. If the clues are not clear to you, ask them. Most importantly, accept that the burden is on the influencer to "know their audience" and not on the audience to follow the influencer blindly.*

FINAL TIP

Organizational Hardware and Software

When we speak about **organizational hardware,** we are thinking about concrete tools, processes, and policies that are created to bring organization, structure, and cadence to the business, its leaders and processes. Organization charts, operational/strategic plans, budgets, procedure manuals, core values, and formal communications are all examples of "organizational hardware." When we speak of **organizational software,** we are thinking about the organizational intangibles — informal connections and influencing styles, cultural influences, informal leadership, traditions, and operating norms. Organizations need both "hardware and software" to function effectively. Our work has consistently shown us that while the more powerful change levers are the "organizational software" levers, leaders and organizations still tend to over-rely on organizational hardware.

Consider making a list of the "organizational hardware" and the "organizational software" you over-rely on as you lead. If you see that you are over-relying on "organizational hardware" make a list of some of the "software" levers you can commit to adopting. Where can you add the critical software levers that will enable you to connect and influence more meaningfully and effectively?

Most importantly, accept that the burden is on the influencer to "know their audience" and not on the audience to follow the influencer blindly.

Adapting Your Style To Meaningfully Connect
TOOL PRACTICE:

Reflect on the section you have just completed.

1. What is your current perspective?

_____

_____

_____

_____

_____

2. How must you shift your perspective to achieve your goal?

_____

_____

_____

_____

_____

3. What leadership prescriptive actions would you take?

_____

_____

_____

_____

_____

CHAPTER EIGHT

Exploring Differences Through Creative Connections

The competitive advantage for a company is lost when its leaders cannot learn to appreciate the creativity that is born from differences in thinking. Leaders who actively seek to explore differences significantly increase their opportunity to strengthen their formal and informal connections across the business and advance the interests of the company. By engaging in constructive debate and being willing to explore problems from different perspectives, leaders can help teams and organizations connect to surface more comprehensive and creative solutions.

One of the reasons leaders avoid leveraging the diversity of thinking is because it involves some degree of discomfort, discord, or even conflict — especially when some enthusiastically lobby for their point of view. Many leaders are not comfortable with conflict. Some leaders hold back their perspective in favor of harmony. Some give in to an early compromise, in support of a quick resolution. Others invest heavily in their own "right" solution and stall the progress.

Those who are adept at conflict management rely on the *third solution*. This is a solution that no one brings into the conflict as "their position," but it emerges as a solution that is co-generated by all participants. The *third solution* is the result produced when the participants align on the essence of the problem and generate together a new and creative solution that suits the needs of the business. The leadership challenge in Exploring Differences Through Creative Connections is to avoid the win-lose solution or the compromise lose-lose solution and to find the win-win, or the **third solution**.

At the core of the leadership tool, **Exploring Differences through Creative Connections** is the ability to lead the right people to co-create a win-win solution that leverages the best of their different perspectives and advances the business.

There are several foundational talents and abilities required to use this tool effectively:

- Ensure that all parties share an aligned view of the business problem before entertaining suggested solutions.
- Actively listen to the differences in others' thinking, while staying in inquiry and suspending judgments.
- Engage in a creative collaboration to generate win-win solutions.

COACHING TIPS

DIAL INTO	DIAL-UP	DIAL-DOWN
Are all parties aligned on a shared view of the business problem?	Unwillingness to move the discussion forward without alignment on the business problem under consideration.	The tendency to move immediately to generate solutions.
Active listening: Is this a talent for you?	Actions you can take to ensure that you are actively listening.	Listening for an opportunity to present and strengthen your argument.
Participative understanding: Are you willing to "own" your accountability as a listener?	• Testing for understanding. • Restating what you believe the other has said or by asking questions.	The immediate and automatic voices of judgment.
Win-win or *Third Solution*: Are you comfortable with this concept?	Leading and facilitating co-generated ideas to solve for a win-win or *Third Solution*.	"I win, and you lose because I am right, and you are wrong."

SUZIE'S STORY

The Choice to Lead

Although few enjoy it, conflict is often beneficial and necessary to advance the best interests of the organization. Suzie had some of the most advanced skills we have ever seen for managing and leveraging conflict. Once, when she was working with a CEO, who did not like to hear unfavorable news, Suzie saved the moment and built a bridge to the future by leveraging conflict. After hearing the results of the executive assessments for his team and the recommendations for intervention proposed by Suzie, the CEO became angry and defensive. Suzie first crossed to his side of the table so that she was seated next to him instead of across from him. She then read from the same sheet as he — calmly correcting his misunderstandings and misinterpretations. Finally, Suzie asked the CEO what problems he saw with the recommendations. She drew out that he was more concerned about the proposed next steps than the content of the assessments. Once Suzie ensured that she and the CEO were aligned on the problem they were solving, they worked together to create different next steps and agreed on a plan. The CEO implemented her recommendations, and the leadership team grew more aligned and powerful together.

Leveraging "Hidden Talents"

It is hard to know with certainty which skills came naturally to Suzie and which skills she learned through practice because she was so mature in her development as a leader. It is likely that she naturally gravitated toward facts, data, logic, and reason; that she stayed objective and detached as she approached situations that could become contentious. She may have been inclined to "take sides," but she disciplined herself instead to listen actively and to "be all sides" — to allow, encourage and personally hold divergent positions and to explore them for creative solutions. Such a level of discipline took a degree of patience that continued to be a developmental challenge for her; nonetheless, she disciplined herself to find her patience in these situations. In doing so, she also mastered the art of the Third Solution. By learning to ensure that the conversation focused on the commonly held problems and encouraging an open and non-judgmental discussion, she consistently removed the "Win-Lose" competition from the space and was indeed able to explore differences through creative connections.

It Starts with Perspective

Suzie changed her perspective, designed a prescription that enabled her to find her hidden talents, remedy her problem, and reach new leadership performance heights.

SUZIE'S PERSPECTIVE SHIFT

Become a leader who creates connections that leverage diversity.

LEADERSHIP PRESCRIPTION

Align on the problem to be solved.
Quiet inclination to either try to "force" a position or to compromise on an answer.
Seek new and creative solutions that work for all and advance the business.

PERFORMANCE

Suzie and the CEO successfully implemented all recommendations, and the team addressed their leadership issues.

One More Note About Suzie

Suzie chose to become an inclusive leader who leveraged the diversity of thinking in a way that advanced the business. Because of her leadership, the company culture was enriched with the spirit of the true diversity of ideas and thought and noted by several outside organizations for her work.

OVER AND UNDER-EMPHASIS ON THIS TOOL

When Too Much Emphasis is on Exploring Differences for Creative Connections

Some leaders are so focused on preserving relationships through differences that they risk compromising the best interests of the business. They tend to allow decisions to stall to avoid or at least delay conflict. Sometimes, they find themselves abandoning their opinions that they regard as sound and in the best interests of the business for the sake of avoiding the perceived risk of conflict or contention. Somehow, they lose sight of the business needs in those moments and lean into preserving the harmony of the relationships. Feedback from their ecosystem typically suggests that these leaders are "conflict-averse" or "indecisive."

> ***Does this sound like you or someone you are coaching?*** *If you are leaning too far into preserving relationships, harmony, or peace, you are likely compromising the overall interests of the business. Again, the* **Third Solution** *is an excellent technique for resolving conflict, which we encourage you to consider practicing. However, if you are coming across as "indecisive" or "not stepping up," we encourage you to find your voice. Keep listening to the views of others but practice integrating their input by playing it back and then advancing the discussion with your agreement, disagreement, or proposals.*

When Too Little Emphasis is on Exploring Differences for Creative Connections

Some leaders become so committed to "being right" that they lose sight of the creative solutions that are available to more powerfully advance the overall interests of the business. They get lost in their argument, believing that the best and only resolution is for the other person to back down or compromise. They are even willing to sacrifice relationships for the taste of victory. Feedback from their ecosystem frequently suggests that these leaders "break too much glass" and are "too invested in being right."

> *Does this sound like you or someone you are coaching? You could be winning the day but losing ground in the long term. Find opportunities to look at the problem in collaboration with others rather than elaborating on your solution. The **Third Solution** is a great technique. Consider practicing it when faced with conflict or contentious challenges: dial-up collaboration and dial down elaboration.*

FINAL TIP

"The Answer" or "An Answer"

Many leaders enter discussions armed with what they believe to be **the answer**. When someone comes to a discussion insisting, they have "the answer," they may be viewed as having called for the discussion under pretenses. What is the purpose of a discussion that begins with "the answer?" Isn't that more like lobbying for support? Starting with **the answer** can shut down the co-authored idea generation that is at the essence of good collaboration and sub-optimizes group problem-solving. We encourage those leaders to shift the narrative inside their heads from "I have *the answer*" to "I may have an idea for **an answer.**" We also encourage leaders to begin all discussions to solve problems with a clear description of the problem that is under consideration and confirmation that everyone in the conversation has the same problem set in mind. With that confirmation, it is OK to move on to look for answers together.

The **Third Solution** is a great technique. Consider practicing it when faced with conflict or contentious problems: dial-up collaboration and dial down elaboration.

Exploring Differences Through Creative Connections
TOOL PRACTICE:

Reflect on the section you have just completed.

1. What is your current perspective?

_____

_____

_____

_____

_____

2. How must you shift your perspective to achieve your goal?

_____

_____

_____

_____

_____

3. What leadership prescriptive actions would you take?

_____

_____

_____

_____

_____

PART THREE:
TOOLS FOR ENSURING ALIGNED IMPLEMENTATION

"Coming together is a beginning; keeping together is progress; working together is success."

EDWARD EVERETT HALE

Flawless implementation is an imperative — not a "nice to have." Many times, implementations stall when leadership teams cannot align on some aspect of the implementation plan. Some leaders receive feedback that they "are too slow to implement" while others that they "have not completely thought through their implementation plans." Some hear that they are too "silo-focused" while others that their plans are "too corporate policy and procedure-focused." Some delay because they have not learned to delegate or leverage others, and they become "bottlenecks" for implementation progress. Others, continually seeking perfection, never seem to launch their projects or products. What they have in common is that very few understand what their feedback means or how to put it into action.

When facing the challenge of aligned implementation, the first step is to ensure a sufficiently broad perspective. Leaders must first shift their perspective from "everyone will do what they agreed to do" to "I will align the system to ensure flawless execution." Leaders must learn to distinguish between *agreement* and *alignment* — what each means and what each takes to create and sustain. An agreement is a sentiment, recognizable through head nods and affirming words. Alignment is a commitment, recognizable through behavioral change that advances a common cause. It does not take much work to build agreement, but alignment is hard work to produce and harder work to sustain.

Alignment is a crucial component of flawless execution. Aligned organizations are beautiful to watch — like a soccer team playing a perfect game. When an organization is aligned, its people have a common goal and a clear direction. They move with velocity and with few flaws even as they execute the most elaborate plans. With this perspective as their new lens, the next step is to write themselves a prescription — a plan to achieve their leadership goal.

Our work with leaders over the past decades confirmed a set of leadership tools that those who successfully lead into the future have learned to prescribe and employ effectively. In this section, we tell stories about leaders who prescribed for themselves strategies and plans to maximize collaboration, ensure alignment, and enable flawless execution across the business:

- Aria, a leadership development officer who achieved extraordinary advances in management practices by **Forwarding the Action to Advance the Business.**
- Dan, a highly popular sales leader who changed the perspective of the salesforce by **Leading to Maximize the Business Enterprise.**
- Kayla, an incredibly resourceful leader who became skilled at **Leveraging Others to Enhance Personal Effectiveness.**
- Peter, a leader who transformed his perspective from "doing perfect work" to **Valuing Good Enough Work.**

CHAPTER NINE

Forwarding The Action To Advance The Business

It is no secret that in today's rapidly changing and dynamic marketplace, speed to market is a competitive advantage, but organizations that focus on speed alone are missing half of the equation. Organizational speed, without direction, can create chaos and re-work; and organizational direction without speed, can generate churn and missed opportunities. Successful leaders learn the art of moving with velocity — the right balance of speed and aligned direction.

We believe that almost all leaders have some experience with teams who engage in unproductive problem-solving discussions where the team tries valiantly to reach decisions either focused on speed or direction alone, and they continually fall short. Often, all on the team participate by offering their solutions, but those solutions are frequently unrelated to one another. This all too common scenario yields discussions that are unproductive and do not reach conclusions to advance the business agenda.

At the core of the leadership tool, **Forwarding the Action to Advance the Business** is the ability to align others on the problem to be solved, on an effective process to solve it, and ultimately, a solution — and to do so with velocity.

There are several foundational talents and abilities required to use this tool effectively:

- Recognize patterns of behaviors that enhance the team alignment process.
- Invest a sufficient amount of time to lead the team to alignment.
- Balance the need for speed with direction.

COACHING TIPS

DIAL INTO	DIAL-UP	DIAL-DOWN
Team Process: How effectively does your team collaborate, decide, and implement together — balancing speed with direction?	The willingness to lead and facilitate the team process to maximize the balance of speed and direction.	A tendency to assume that team discussions will lead to aligned conclusions.
The Problem: How can you ensure that all team members are aligned on the problem before they start to solve it?	Leadership and facilitative actions that test for alignment on the problem.	The tendency to start solving before the problem is clear to all.
The Action: How will you know when it is time to forward the action?	• Ensure that everyone is "heard." • Listening and watching for commitment. • Willingness to stop the process to re-build alignment.	A tendency to underestimate how much *team process* work is required to create and maintain team alignment.

ARIA'S STORY

The Choice to Lead

There is an almost predictable tendency for leadership teams to spend hours engaged in problem-solving discussions that are unproductive and do not inform any decisions. Team members vie for airtime, and each advances their ideas that do not necessarily build on or even relate to each other. The result: the team makes no decision, the progress of the team stalls, and they do not advance the business agenda.

Aria always set her sights on a better leadership outcome. In her role as vice president of leadership development, she led her team through the unenviable task of aligning twelve of her peer human resources vice presidents to support a very disciplined approach to managing performance and differentiating compensation awards. Further complicating the challenge, each of her peers worked for a different business leader who had very definite and conflicting ideas about distinguishing performance and pay. They mostly wanted to continue the age-old practice of paying everyone by some formula that did not require them to explain why they awarded more to some than to others.

Aria knew that she had the full support of the CEO to implement her process, but she also knew from experience how poorly a forced process change would be received and performed. So, she adjusted her targeted outcome from just implementing a process to implementing one that stakeholders owned and supported. This adjustment called for a set of talents that did not come naturally to her. Aria met weekly with her peers. At each meeting, she ensured that they aligned on the problem they were solving and the actions they would take to solve it. She never let the decisions languish, nor did she allow them to be prematurely adopted. She resolved one hurdle at a time — listening to their input and working to find creative solutions. She literally, "took her peers with her" as she developed her process. Aria collaborated on the goals of the process, the design, and the implementation plan and forwarded the action. Once launched, this process was highly effective at building higher organizational performance, and it also enjoyed full system support.

Leveraging "Hidden Talents"

The ability to lead alignment across competing agendas sometimes takes the patient willingness to "first go slow to finish fast," not natural talents or inclinations for Aria. Aria loved to be in action and progressing toward business goals. She disciplined herself to lead with a balance of speed (her natural inclination) and patient direction. She learned to value the quality of the thinking that the team unleashed through the process of resolving tension points — creating a scenario where team members knew they were heard and they were genuinely co-designing the complete process. Her leadership style ensured their buy-in, alignment, and ownership. With all her standards for collaboration satisfied, she shifted back into results mode and moved the group beyond cooperation to forwarding the action with velocity.

It Starts with Perspective

Aria changed her perspective, designed a prescription that enabled her to find her hidden talents to remedy her problem and to reach new leadership performance heights.

ARIA'S PERSPECTIVE SHIFT

> Become a leader who continually forwards the action with velocity in service of the business agenda.

Quiet any inclination to assume that team facilitation will happen on its own without working on it.
Take specific actions to ensure that each team speaks and that team members listen well. Avoid distractions.
Practice continually watching for the signs that the team is falling out of alignment — quiet people, body language, passive language — and stop the action to re-build alignment when necessary.

PERFORMANCE

Aria's ability to lead a cross-organizational team effectively allowed the organization to implement a state of the art performance and reward platform.

One More Note About Aria

Aria chose to become a leader who continually advanced the best interests of the business and enjoyed extraordinary success as a subject matter expert who flawlessly implemented plans and programs throughout the enterprise. Her ability to lead cross-organizationally allowed her to change her "brand" from subject matter expert to organizational leadership. She went on to become a successful entrepreneur and an active board member and leader.

OVER AND UNDER-EMPHASIS ON THIS TOOL

When Too Much Emphasis is on Forwarding the Action to Advance the Business

Some leaders think that it takes too much time and wastes too much energy to build team buy-in and alignment. They believe that they know what to do, and including others would delay their progress. Sometimes others refer to them as "expedient" or even "the Maverick." They make quick and independent progress initially but often stall when key stakeholders insert themselves into the process. Feedback from their ecosystem typically suggests that these leaders are "not collaborative" or "not team players."

>*Does this sound like you or someone you are coaching?* *Consider dialing up your focus on teamwork and collaboration leadership. Your inclination toward action, balanced with inclusive decision making is a potent combination. Your inclination toward speed is best when coupled with a focused direction that comes with aligning critical stakeholders with the common goals and objectives. You will likely be slowed down eventually by these very same stakeholders that you have omitted from the process. Once you have aligned the key stakeholders, then you can move forward in action to advance the business agenda.*

When Too Little Emphasis is on Forwarding the Action to Advance the Business

Some leaders are so focused on the direction they believe best advances the business that they do not make room for others in their problem-solving process — neither taking the time to align on the specific challenge to be solved nor opening themselves up to hear the possible solutions and ideas that others offer. The result is that they cannot lead the group to an aligned solution. Instead, their decision process stalls or they can leave the room, believing that they have alignment when they do not, and there are no follow up actions. Their meetings may end without clear accountabilities or decisions. As a result, they likely do not advance the work. Feedback from their ecosystem typically suggests that these leaders are slow to implement or drive to a conclusion.

>*Does this sound like you or someone you are coaching?* *Consider dialing up the value you place on the team alignment*

process before pre-determining a direction — which involves a willingness and an appropriate level of patience for listening to the direction and ideas of others and a willingness to give up the notion that your course is the best and only path forward. If you are too heavily invested in your way forward, you risk losing the followership required to achieve the results you desire. Worse, you may think you have created followership, rely on it, and fail to forward the action and advance the business agenda.

FINAL TIP

Why is the question, "what problem are we solving" so important?

When it comes to forwarding the action of an organization or leading continual progress, the question, **what problem are we solving?** can be a valuable tool for collaborative problem-solving. The following story illustrates why.

A CEO was concerned that people in the organizational level beneath his direct reports seemed disconnected and distant from him. He decided that he wanted to host a party for that group. He shared his idea with his direct reports but offered no context — just his desire to host a party. His direct reports immediately began sharing their ideas for the party that were unrelated to the CEO's purpose. As the discussion continued unproductively, the CEO became frustrated and abandoned his plan. Had he articulated the object and the problem he was trying to solve, the conversation would have been more productive.

Without a clear and common purpose, meetings, and discussions meander. Why? When leaders initiate conversations absent a clear and common goal or problem statement, assumptions take over. As each participant operates inside of their own set of assumptions, their contributions become unrelated, and the discussion becomes unfocused and unproductive.

Productive collaborations that advance the business have one thing in common: a clear purpose and problem statement that aligns the group. Clear explanations of purpose and problem help us forward the action. If meetings begin "to churn," ask the question, ***what problem are we solving?***

Productive collaborations that advance the business have one thing in common: a clear purpose and problem statement that aligns the group. Clear explanations of purpose and problem help us forward the action. If meetings begin "to churn," ask the question, *what problem are we solving?*

Forwarding The Action To Advance The Business
TOOL PRACTICE:

Reflect on the section you have just completed.

1. What is your current perspective?

_____

_____

_____

_____

_____

2. How must you shift your perspective to achieve your goal?

_____

_____

_____

_____

_____

3. What leadership prescriptive actions would you take?

_____

_____

_____

_____

_____

CHAPTER TEN

Leading To Maximize
The Business Enterprise

In a centralized business, all the power and, hence, all the decisions flow upward to a single source, which is usually a leadership team. If business segments are part of the dynamic, the balance between a sole corporate entity focus and a business segment focus becomes paramount. If one then adds the dynamic of functional areas of expertise to the already matrixed environment, the plot thickens. Who is in charge? Which areas of the business take priority? These questions loom large in the minds of many leaders.

There is no question about the importance of a passionate commitment to customers, but when the needs and desires of customers conflict with the best interests of the business, that passion can become disruptive. The same is the case if the needs and desires of any business segment or function come into conflict with the overall good of the enterprise. Successful leaders learn to maximize the interests of the business enterprise as a whole while optimizing the needs of the various segments. These leaders can raise their thinking above the level of their personal or silo needs and focus first on serving the enterprise as a whole.

At the core of the leadership tool, *Leading to Maximize the Business Enterprise* is the ability to understand the implications of decisions in light of the entire enterprise business and to make prudent decisions that ultimately serve the best interests of all with the right degree of balance and trade-offs.

There are some foundational talents and abilities required to use this tool effectively:

- Understand the system of connections and controls that drive the business — the enterprise, its segments, and functions.
- Connect and align leaders who have to compete for resources through the governance system.
- Lead through the conflicts involved with making trade-off decisions that best advance the enterprise.

COACHING TIPS

DIAL INTO	DIAL-UP	DIAL-DOWN
The total business system: What are the parts and how are they interconnected?	Knowledge of the business, its segments and functions, and the principal objectives of each.	The assumption that the hierarchy and formal organizational channels are sufficient for balanced management.
The enterprise priorities: Where are the points of contention across the enterprise? Where will possible tradeoffs be required?	• Areas of frequent contention across the enterprise. • What has worked to resolve these points of contention in the past?	The tendency to react to fix an issue in isolation without regard for the implications across the enterprise.
Maximizing for the total enterprise first: What are the "tight" (uniform across all business segments) priorities and decisions?	The "tight" areas of control that are in question — values, strategy, positive business results.	Any tendency to over or under-emphasize the enterprise as a whole.
Optimizing for the parts: What are the "loose" priorities and decisions (what is customizable by the segments and does not compromise the overall enterprise).	The "loose" areas of control that are in question — prudent risk-taking, innovation, entrepreneurial requirements?	Any tendency to over or under-emphasize the segments of the enterprise.
Governance: What is the system of governance that resolves issues?	How do you leverage the governance system to resolve business issues?	Using rank or position to resolve issues.

DAN'S STORY

The Choice to Lead

Dan inherited a sales organization that had distanced itself from the rest of the organizational stakeholders and had become a financial burden after years of high expenses and low profits. The relationships between the sales force and their colleagues throughout the business enterprise were strained, and support was minimal. When Dan became the leader, he recognized the problems inherent in the lack of support for the sales organization and determined it necessary to build more positive connections between his organization and the rest of the company. He used his natural sales talents to guide him as he set out to solidify the bonds between sales and the other segments of the business that sales relied upon for partnership and support. Dan's leadership goal was to ensure that each part of the "organizational ecosystem" committed their full and best efforts to support the sales team, in service of customer support and business success. The result was tight relationships and alignment, the velocity of process flow, and improved profitability for the entire business.

Leveraging "Hidden Talents"

Dan was always a passionate customer advocate. However, as he grew in seniority and experience, so did his knowledge of the business, its strategy, and its balance sheet. Dan found himself too often fixing the problems that materialized when the sales team focused more on short-term orders than long-term profits. He recognized that his tendency to advocate for the customer was not always good enterprise stewardship. So, Dan sought to strike a better balance of advocacy between the customer and the enterprise. When he asked himself what that would take from his leadership, he concluded that his priority had to be the business enterprise and that he was going to need to develop more comfort with disagreement and conflict that was required to achieve this right balance. Dan trained himself to think about the ramifications to the business enterprise first — that was the easy part. When the enterprise needs were not in concert with the needs of the customer, Dan trained himself to remain resolute in his advocacy for the business enterprise as a whole — despite the protests of his sales team. With the needs of the enterprise satisfied, Dan could then turn his attention toward supporting the needs of the sales team and customers to the best of his ability.

It Starts with Perspective

Dan changed his perspective, designed a prescription that enabled him to find his hidden talents, remedy his problem, and reach new leadership performance heights.

DAN'S PERSPECTIVE SHIFT

Become a leader for the whole of the business enterprise.

LEADERSHIP PRESCRIPTION

Practice reflecting upon areas of recurring contention between the needs of the customer and the needs of the enterprise — and proactively plan for them.

Log the likely areas of contention that most compete with the business enterprise priorities.

Tolerate the contention involved with pushing back on the sales team when it is appropriate to prioritize the needs of the enterprise.

PERFORMANCE

Dan found the right balance between maximizing for the business enterprise and optimizing for the customer in a way that drove profitability.

One More Note About Dan

Dan chose to become a leader for the whole business and pre-scribed actions to achieve that goal. He became so adept at his ability to see the needs of the "whole of the business enterprise" as well as the business functions and to make the right adjust-ments and trade-offs to provide maximum advantages to both, that he moved from the sales leadership track to the CEO track. He enjoyed enormous success.

OVER AND UNDER-EMPHASIS ON THIS TOOL

When Leading to Maximize the Business Enterprise is Over-Emphasized

Some leaders tend toward advocating for the safest path — the policy, the hierarchy, the over-inclusive decision process that can slow the business to a crawl, trudging through the bureaucratic process and "red tape" of the enterprise. Often, so many leaders find their way into the enterprise decision-making processes that it becomes hard to determine who is accountable for the decision. Unfortunately, while fighting it out among themselves, they forget about the needs of the customer. Feedback from their ecosystem typically suggests that these leaders avoid risk, organizational contention, accountability, or mistakes.

> *Does this sound like you or someone you are coaching?* *Consider the irony of this model — by over-rotating to the concerns of the business enterprise, we risk its efficiency and effectiveness.* **When business leaders cannot make timely decisions, they place the company at risk.** *When en-terprise leaders create difficult process hurdles, the business cannot make appropriate choices. Instead, practice challenging yourself to identify the key areas that are "tight" and those that are "loose." With that in mind: Who are the key stakeholders who must be involved in the decision? Who needs to approve? Use that list and those categories to manage the required steps.*

When Leading to Maximize the Business Enterprise is Under-Emphasized

"Mavericks" seem to move quickly but have a way of finding roadblocks along the path. Their overarching goal seems to be whatever they are personally advocating — whatever they or their business segments deem most important. They can count on resistance any time they take action that impacts other stakeholders in the system without affording them the appropriate avenues to advocate for their needs and wants. Feedback from their ecosystem suggests that they are too silo-focused and insufficiently focused on the overall business.

> *Does this sound like you or someone you are coaching? Consider the jeopardy of such a personal model. You will meet resistance, rejection, or harsh criticism if you move to action without taking your decision stakeholders with you. After making some early progress, you will likely stall. Very frequently, stakeholders appear aligned during the discussion phase and resist during the implementation phase. Identify the stakeholders, understand their needs, and turn them into advocates for the decision before implementation.*

FINAL TIP

To Maximize or to Optimize?

When we speak about *maximizing*, we are thinking about producing the highest desired result. If we talk about *optimizing*, we are thinking about finding the most suitable solution set available. These are quite different. Successful leaders most often find their answers by looking through the lens of maximizing the total interests of the business enterprise first and then focusing on the most effective means of strengthening the segments of the enterprise. For example, the sales force works toward maximizing profits while optimizing the sales tools, training, and support available to the sales leaders, although circumstances might occasionally inform a different decision. Effective leaders understand and manage these tradeoffs effectively — with their eye always trained on ensuring aligned implementation and advancing the interests of the entire business.

Successful leaders most often find their answers by looking through the lens of maximizing the total interests of the business enterprise first and then focusing on the most effective means of strengthening the segments of the enterprise.

Leading To Maximize The Business Enterprise
TOOL PRACTICE:

Reflect on the section you have just completed.

1. What is your current perspective?

_____

_____

_____

_____

_____

2. How must you shift your perspective to achieve your goal?

_____

_____

_____

_____

_____

3. What leadership prescriptive actions would you take?

_____

_____

_____

_____

_____

CHAPTER ELEVEN

Leveraging Others To Enhance Personal Effectiveness

Although many leaders receive feedback that they cannot effectively "multi-task," experts in the field of leadership development question the accuracy and even the wisdom of such feedback. Perhaps the better question, is how effectively the leader is advancing multiple streams of work concurrently? That question calls up the distinction between *doing versus leveraging others*. Many of us cannot effectively do numerous things at once; but, all leaders have the option to develop a talent for leveraging others to enable them to advance various streams of work concurrently.

When leaders receive feedback that they cannot effectively advance multiple streams of work concurrently, it likely means that they prefer to operate sequentially and exclusively — driving one task at a time. Ironically, this tendency may have served them well earlier in their career, but in jobs with broader scopes, this preference to operate sequentially can become a liability.

At the core of the leadership tool, **Leveraging Others To Enhance Personal Effectiveness** is the ability to oversee and advance various streams of work concurrently and in alignment with others.

There are several foundational talents and abilities required to use this tool effectively:

- Recognize and lead the right people, to the right place at the right time to produce the desired result.
- Develop a working knowledge of the accountabilities of others across the organization.
- Enroll and lead others in virtual teams.
- Develop follow-up skills and "closed loops" with key stakeholders.

COACHING TIPS

DIAL INTO	DIAL-UP	DIAL-DOWN
Requirements for Flawless Implementation: What are they?	• Desired outcomes. • Required results. • Individuals to leverage.	• A tendency to rely on formal organization relationships to ensure implementation. • Ad hoc approach to implementation.
Organizational Awareness: Who are the right, accountable people?	How to get the right people focused on the right things by the appointed time to implement flawlessly.	A tendency to do it oneself.
Are you willing to leverage others and hold them accountable?	Influencing participation and holding team members accountable.	Holding others accountable through rank or hierarchy.
Stakeholder Communication: Who requires what information?	• Status reports. • Follow-up loops. • Collaboration.	A tendency to under-communicate.

KAYLA'S STORY

The Choice to Lead

Through the years, we have heard many leaders say, "I need to clone myself to get all my work done." The problem is that frequently, too many things can require different degrees of a leader's attention — too many things with too little time. Kayla never figured out how to solve the problem of "cloning herself," but she did figure out how to extend herself. She was part of the executive recruiting organization. The team was made up of all individual contributors, and they had no assigned administrative assistants. One day, due to last-minute scheduling changes, three prospective board member candidates were scheduled to interview with several officers. This day had to run flawlessly. She created an ad hoc team, asking each member to help with specific tasks while staying within their permanently assigned roles: greet the candidates, provide them with schedules and call the designated "tour guides" to meet them. She enlisted the officers' assistants to serve as those guides. She sought help from the human resources generalists to gather feedback, while she led other aspects of the day as a conductor would lead a symphony. She did this while keeping her bosses and stakeholders comfortably in the loop. The day ran flawlessly, as did all cross-organizational implementations under her leadership.

Leveraging "Hidden Talents"

Kayla had excellent skills for managing across multiple tasks and initiatives. Early in her career, she assured quality work with her laser-like "mono-focus," — or focusing on one task or project from start to finish, a style that came naturally to her. As her career advanced, she was forced to become "multi-focused," while still assuring high-quality work, often indicating that she needed to "clone herself" — which is what she practically taught herself to do. There was nothing about enlisting and engaging others to help her accomplish the goals that came naturally to her. Out of necessity, she developed three critical abilities to ensure her success:

- Ask for help.
- Appropriately leverage organizational colleagues.
- Keep key stakeholders informed.

She managed stakeholder expectations and team progress. She checked-in with critical stakeholders all along the way, and she never disappointed. Kayla extended her reach to almost "clone herself," and she leveraged others to enhance her effectiveness.

It Starts with Perspective

Kayla changed her perspective, designed a prescription that enabled her to find her hidden talents, remedy her problem, and reach new leadership performance heights.

KAYLA'S PERSPECTIVE SHIFT

Become a leader who enhances effectiveness by leveraging others.

LEADERSHIP PRESCRIPTION

Note the work required to complete tasks, projects, or programs, and who are the most likely individuals to enroll in planning and implementation.

Adapt style to influence and enroll the right people in the implementation.

Clarify goals, objectives, and timelines — and frequently discuss progress.

PERFORMANCE

The board recruiting day ran flawlessly, as did all cross-organizational implementations under her leadership.

One More Note About Kayla

Kayla became a leader who enhanced her effectiveness by leveraging others. This tool, which she frequently employed, enabled her to cover more territory and allowed her to deliver the flawless implementation of the day's events with exceptional quality.

OVER AND UNDER-EMPHASIS ON THIS TOOL

When Too Much Emphasis is on Leveraging Others to Enhance Personal Effectiveness

Some leaders tend to randomly focus on various streams of work and count on others to implement. They tend to dive into the middle of projects, start and stop them and move among several projects at the same time — they may even allow project deadlines to slip or fall between the cracks. They can create "disruption" within the organization as they follow an "ad hoc" style. Feedback from their ecosystem typically suggests that these leaders' "are inconsistent, their style is often disruptive, and they struggle to implement."

> ***Does this sound like you or someone you are coaching?***
> *You may have some tendencies toward an unstructured implementation style. If you can implement successfully and more comfortably in a less structured way, ensure that your success does not come with the too-high cost to others who are impacted by your style. If you notice that some of your work is falling out of scope, consider visually displaying the status of all projects in your total portfolio. It is also essential to keep the status of projects under your direction available to the stakeholders.*

When Too Little Emphasis is on Leveraging Others to Enhance Personal Effectiveness

Some leaders prefer to focus sequentially and exclusively on the specific requirements of each piece of a project. They likely address one project at a time from start to finish. They probably know the organization and the individuals to call upon to help them implement, but they do not choose to leverage them. Feedback from their ecosystem typically suggests that these leaders are singularly focused and not managing the other parts of their work portfolio.

> ***Does this sound like you or someone you are coaching?*** *Consider visually displaying the status of all projects in your total portfolio to ensure that nothing critical falls out of view while your focus diverts to the next requirement you are implementing. You may have to practice lifting yourself into more of an oversight position so that you can keep your many streams of work in your sights while you select where to apply your focus.*

FINAL TIP

Doing Versus Leveraging Others

One of the hardest transitions for leaders to make as they start to advance through executive levels is the transition from ***"doing"*** things themselves to ***"leveraging others"*** to do them. Through the years, we heard many excuses ... "it's easier to do it myself" ... "I know I should but don't have the time ..." and many more. Thinking that you can do it all is risky and may become career-limiting as your responsibilities grow. Eventually, people who try to do too much become "gatekeepers" and roadblocks who slow the progress of the organization. If you are reluctant to *leverage others*, try this simple exercise as a first step.

Ask your team to help you create three lists:

1) Things you are doing that others could or should be able to do independent of you.
2) Things that you are doing that others could or should be able to do with a little help from you.
3) Things you currently do that others could take on if you taught them.

One of the hardest transitions for leaders to make when they start to advance through executive levels is the transition from "doing" things themselves to "leveraging others" to do them.

Leveraging Others to Enhance Personal Effectiveness
TOOL PRACTICE:

Reflect on the section you have just completed.

1. What is your current perspective?

_____

_____

_____

_____

2. How must you shift your perspective to achieve your goal?

_____

_____

_____

_____

3. What leadership prescriptive actions would you take?

_____

_____

_____

_____

CHAPTER TWELVE

Valuing "Good Enough" Work

Leaders who seek perfection appear to find more success early in their careers than later. They produce high-quality work without much help from others, so they are highly valued, richly rewarded, and rapidly advanced through the organization. As their portfolio expands, their standards for perfection can become a liability within the organization. As they advance, their work becomes more interdependent than independent — with others depending upon their work to complete their own. Perfection can lead to stalled progress and organizational "bottlenecking." Successful leaders learn to adopt the "Good Enough Standard," the right balance between the need for perfection and the need for progress. The leadership challenge in *Valuing Good Enough Work* is to learn that balance and apply it appropriately.

At the core of the leadership tool, **Valuing Good Enough Work** is the ability to learn this balance and apply it appropriately.

There are several foundational talents and abilities required to use this tool effectively:

- Recognize the essential elements needed for success.
- Willingness to negotiate deadlines and success requirements with stakeholders.
- Courage to accept "good enough work" as complete.

COACHING TIPS

DIAL INTO	DIAL-UP	DIAL-DOWN
Success: What are the essential elements of this project or implementation?	A keen and accurate sense of what "good enough" may look like in this particular case.	A tendency toward perfection.
Alignment of stakeholders: How do you align all with success criteria?	A keen and accurate sense of the right people to involve in the process of setting success criteria.	The tendency to decide within the silo and not to build alignment across the organization.
Personal courage: How do you align yourself with success criteria?	The bests interests of the business.	Fear of failure.

PETER'S STORY

The Choice to Lead: Peter's Story

Peter's spin-off business was in its preliminary stages. Processes were not yet available, nor were subject matter experts. Half the sales force on staff for the spin-off business were from the parent company, and half were new hires. The former suffered change fatigue; the latter were too recently hired to their roles to be productive. The sales leader was anxious to invest in training, but first, he had to understand the skills outages and training needs. He asked Peter, his human resources partner, to create a sales skills assessment. In time, such support would be available from appropriate subject matter experts, but that was not yet the case. So, Peter had a problem: he had a mission-critical request from the sales leader but no subject matter expertise available to design it and no funds to hire the knowledge from the outside.

Peter saw a "roughly right" solution. After aligning all the right stakeholders on his project specifications, Peter went into action — he interviewed some of the most skilled sales leaders, held a focus group of customers, incorporated the corporate values and created a temporary sales skills model. The sales leaders assessed all members of the salesforce against this common set of standards, and the results were used to develop very targeted assessment and training programs. Perfect? Likely no. "Good enough" to accomplish the goal without disrupting the ecosystem? Absolutely!

Leveraging "Hidden Talents"

If Peter followed his inclinations, he would have spent all day every day with clients brainstorming the right solutions for their needs. He loved to generate ideas and then generate some more ideas, always expecting a better one to come to mind. His intuition was a loud voice in his head, suggesting that there was still a better idea — so, he was inclined to work the problem instead of closing on a solution. As Peter's career progressed and his accountabilities grew, he disciplined himself to accept "good enough ideas" and "ideas that would work" as the benchmark in many situations instead of continually seeking something better. By collaborative planning, he was able to structure criteria that helped them screen out many of his ideas and highlight the ones that were "good enough" to solve the problem. He learned to negotiate and codify standards and specifications for project completion. Peter will likely always have a mind filled with more and better ideas, but he has trained himself to listen to the voices of implementation sooner and to see the value of "good enough work" solutions.

It Starts with Perspective

Peter changed his perspective, designed a prescription that enabled him to find his hidden talents, remedy his problem, and reach new leadership performance heights.

PETER'S PERSPECTIVE SHIFT

> Become a leader who continually builds alignment for "good enough" work.

LEADERSHIP PRESCRIPTION

> Identify the essential elements of success for this project or implementation.
>
> Align and set clear standards for success with other key stakeholders.
>
> Quiet the voices calling for perfection and declare that the project is complete.

PERFORMANCE

> He developed a sale training curriculum, specifically targeting the needs of the sales force, resulting in increased sales and productivity.

One More Note About Peter

Peter chose to become a leader who continually built alignment for "good enough" work. He strongly influenced the organization to balance progress over perfection — a cultural shift that had implications outside of his immediate area of responsibility.

OVER AND UNDER-EMPHASIS ON THIS TOOL

When Too Much Emphasis is on Valuing Good Enough Work

Some leaders seek perfection and are challenged to declare a project "finished." They believe that they must work on projects until they are flawless, however insignificant. Feedback from their ecosystem typically suggests that these leaders go through countless revisions and may "sacrifice productivity for perfection."

> *Does this sound like you or someone you are coaching?*
> *Reframe your thinking to accept "a good enough standard." There is too much on your plate to insist on perfection. We encourage you to change your self-talk from "this work is not the quality I am capable of producing" to "this is good enough work." How do we define "good enough work?" It is work that accomplishes all the set goals, meets all objective specifications, is of acceptable enough quality for you to move on and not sacrifice the remainder of your accountabilities. Learn to set "good enough" specifications in advance and accept them when you achieve them.*

When Too Little Emphasis is on Valuing Good Enough Work

Some leaders get bored quickly. There is a certain excitement that is generated by new projects. Some leaders even get bored after new projects meet the most basic specifications, look for the next opportunity, and move on to it. Feedback from their ecosystem typically suggests that these leaders "are inconsistent, too scattered to follow through and often, cannot implement."

> *Does this sound like you or someone you are coaching?*
> *If you are not willing to exert full energy through the project implementation and completion, create some mechanism to*

help yourself do so. Calendar notations or other reminders are easy first steps. Another useful technique is to ensure that you have someone on your team who has natural project management and implementation skills that complement your own. A final point — remember that your accountability does not end until the project concludes.

FINAL TIP

"Roughly Right"

John Maynard Keynes said, "It is better to be roughly right than precisely wrong." Maybe you have heard others reference **roughly right**. We have found that the expression "roughly right" is hard for many leaders to understand and embrace. We prefer the term "good enough work." We define "good enough work" as work that is complete, clear, on time, and acceptable by any objective or reasonable standard. It is of a quality that allows leaders to work smarter, produce more, and not sacrifice one part of the work portfolio for another. Practice this concept, at first on low visibility projects and then, as your confidence and experience on this concept build, extend the idea to more projects as appropriate, according to your judgment.

We define "good enough work" as work that is complete, clear, on time, and acceptable by any objective or reasonable standard. It is of a quality that allows leaders to work smarter, produce more, and not sacrifice one part of the work portfolio for another.

Valuing "Good Enough" Work TOOL PRACTICE:

Reflect on the section you have just completed.

1. What is your current perspective?

_____

_____

_____

_____

_____

2. How must you shift your perspective to achieve your goal?

_____

_____

_____

_____

_____

3. What leadership prescriptive actions would you take?

_____

_____

_____

_____

_____

PART FOUR:
TOOLS FOR PERSONAL LEADERSHIP

It is our choices that show what we truly are far more than our abilities.

J.K. ROWLING

There is always some degree of discomfort inherent in embracing personal growth and development because it involves acknowledging vulnerabilities and taking risks with new and unpracticed behaviors. This discomfort is exacerbated by the vague and confusing feedback that leaders receive as they advance through their careers. Some have received feedback that they "do not own things," and others that they are "too controlling." Some receive feedback that they are "micro-managers" while others that they give their teams, "too much independence." Some leaders are told that they are "rigid'" while others that they lack "self-discipline." Some leaders discern that they "are too overcome by events," and others that they are "too far into the weeds." What they have in common is that very few understand what their feedback means or how to put it into action.

In many cases, embracing this feedback may require that they abandon past styles and preferences that have helped them advance to their current levels. Changing what has always worked may seem counter-productive and require some degree of a leap of faith. This experience is why we have come to believe that the most crucial factor for all leaders in fully embracing personal development is courage. With this perspective as their new lens, the next step is to write themselves a prescription — a plan to achieve their leadership goal.

Our work with leaders over the past decades has confirmed a set of leadership tools that those who successfully developed their leadership have learned to prescribe and employ effectively. In this section, we share stories about leaders who chose to embrace various common leadership challenges and, in the process, helped to strengthen their organization and the overall business.

- Robert, a stable and reliable general manager who was an exemplar for *Living and Leading Commitment and Accountability.*
- David, a highly creative and independent thinker who strengthened his leadership by *Growing Personal Awareness and Self-Management.*
- Monica, an extraordinary executive assistant who became an innovative leader by *Adapting to the Unpredictable Workplace.*
- Dante, a courageous and talented human resources professional who enhanced his effectiveness by *Building and Leading Autonomous Teams.*

CHAPTER THIRTEEN

Living and Leading Commitment and Accountability

Accountability is a popular topic among authors focused on today's workplace. Unfortunately, many leaders are confused and even cynical about the concept. At its core, accountability is about keeping one's word, doing what one has committed, with and for others who are counting on it. If the "forces of the world intervene," and one is unable to deliver what they have committed, it may cease to be their fault, but it remains their accountability. Real accountability is an unbreakable promise. In this regard, authentic accountability is a valuable commodity within any organization.

Others can assign responsibilities, but ***personal accountability is a choice — a choice to make the right commitments to oneself and one's organization and to keep them***. Leaders who embrace this perspective inspire high confidence within the organization.

At the core of the leadership tool, **Living and Leading Accountability** is the commitment to one's word and actions.

There are several foundational talents and abilities required to use this tool effectively:

- Hold oneself to exacting standards of personal commitment.
- Ensure tight alignment of commitment and action.
- Demonstrate the courage to "own" failures.

COACHING TIPS

DIAL INTO	DIAL-UP	DIAL-DOWN
Commitments: What do they mean to you?	The commitments you have made to others and the organization and the implications to each if you do not deliver.	A tendency to assume that trying is enough of a demonstration of commitment.
Your word and your deed: How closely aligned are they?	Past commitments that you have missed and the degree of ownership you have felt and demonstrated.	The tendency to excuse yourself if it "wasn't your fault."

ROBERT'S STORY

The Choice to Lead

The design and administration team of the Sales Compensation Plan at Robert's company had been through multiple leadership changes in a brief period. The plan administration lost the focused attention it needed and with it the oversight, clear guidelines, and the structured implementation required. Most importantly, there was a significant lack of trust in the process as well as in the designers and in the administrators — all of which needed improvement. There was no one with deep sales compensation experience and the right set of skills to take over and restore the credibility of the plan. Still, Robert's name was the first, and the only name surfaced. Even though he had no direct experience working with sales compensation, it was so apparent that he had just the right temperament, finely-honed implementation skills and, most importantly, a reputation for accountability and integrity. He was the right leader to re-establish the credibility of the program and the administration of the sales compensation plan.

Leveraging "Hidden Talents"

Robert was successful in re-establishing the creditability of the sales compensation plan and its administration by keeping steadfastly to all the commitments he made, both large and small. Often, it is the small demonstrations of accountability that make the most lasting impressions, and such was the case with Robert. Each day, he carved out time on his busy schedule to catch up, giving himself a buffer that allowed him to manage the unexpected distractions and be on time for his meetings. Other leaders trusted their schedule with him for so long that he built up credibility to cover those organizational incidents that were beyond his control. When facing calendar conflicts, he learned to reach out to the leaders who were being inconvenienced, apologize, and personally take the lead in re-scheduling — he made no excuses. This individualized touch did not come naturally to Robert, but he learned its importance to others. He also came to see it as another demonstration of keeping his commitment to those around him by "owning" his choices, never "blamestorming" (or brainstorming who to blame) and having the courage to apologize and ask for "do-overs." Robert's small demonstrations of accountability made the most lasting impression and ultimately led others to trust him to restore the integrity of the sales compensation plan administration.

It Starts with Perspective

Robert changed his perspective, designed a prescription that enabled him to find his hidden talents, remedy his problem, and reach new leadership performance heights.

> Become a leader whose word and deed consistently match.

LEADERSHIP PRESCRIPTION

> Quiet the inclination to be defensive in the face of failure or unsatisfactory results.

> Clarify specific commitments before accepting them.

> Keep commitments — if unable to keep a promise, own it, and take the first steps to fix it.

PERFORMANCE

> He restored a sense of authenticity and trust in the sales compensation process while he developed a plan that drove the sales behaviors that advanced the business.

One More Note About Robert

Robert became a leader whose word and deed consistently matched. Although he had to learn quite a bit about sales compensation, he was the leader for the job. Robert restored a sense of authenticity and trust in the process while he developed a plan that drove the sales behaviors that advanced the business results. As a result, he received many other significant assignments outside of his area of expertise over the years.

OVER AND UNDER-EMPHASIS ON THIS TOOL

When Too Much Emphasis is on Living and Leading Commitment and Accountability

It is hard to imagine that someone could put too much emphasis on accountability, but some leaders do just that. They view every organizational outage or breakdown as their accountability to own and resolve. These leaders are both a blessing and a burden to the organization — a blessing for their heightened sense of ownership; a burden because their actions blur the real lines of accountability and shield those who do not step into the areas of accountability they own. Feedback from their ecosystem typically suggests that these leaders are "overextended and overwhelmed."

Does this sound like you or someone you are coaching?
If you or someone you coach find yourselves stepping into every organizational outage or breakdown or volunteering for every project, even when you believe that others own these projects, consider the implications by asking the following questions:

- *Are you unintentionally preventing those who are genuinely accountable for stepping up?*
- *What are the long-term organizational implications of blurring the lines of accountability?*
- *Are you preventing the organization from seeing areas of breakage?*

Your real accountability in these instances is to have the courage to hold the right people accountable.

When Too Little Emphasis is on Living and Leading Commitment and Accountability

Unfortunately, some leaders are uncomfortable assuming accountability. It frequently shows up in behaviors such as deflecting, avoiding, and even blaming. Any such conduct creates a division within the team and drains the energy of the entire group. Feedback from their ecosystem typically suggests that these leaders "do not demonstrate ownership and commitment."

Does this sound like you or someone you are coaching?
If you or someone you are coaching is struggling to own commitments and keep promises, consider changing perspective from "it is not my fault" to "it is my accountability." The former drains you of your power and strength, while the latter builds your energy and vitality. The choice is yours to make.

FINAL TIP

Integrity and Sincerity?

Robert's story suggests a significant and illuminating comparison: when we speak about *sincerity*, we are thinking about leaders who are without pretense, who are transparent and who genuinely mean what they say, at the time they say it. When we speak about *integrity*, we are thinking about those individuals who can be counted on to do what they say — leaders who authentically live their words — all their words and their commitments. It is important to note that *sincerity* is not a leadership flaw, but that *integrity* is a sophisticated leadership trait. Most leaders are sincere, but few are consistently in integrity. The latter takes more deliberate and intentional efforts. As a first step toward developing your integrity awareness, practice monitoring your commitments (i.e., what have you agreed to do for others or yourself, your calendar, your objectives). Each time you see that you are going to miss a commitment, own it, and re-negotiate it. Each time you do not deliver on a promise, acknowledge it. It takes courage to hold yourself accountable to your word.

It is important to note that *sincerity* is not a leadership flaw, but that ***integrity*** is a sophisticated leadership trait. Most leaders are sincere, but few are consistently in integrity. The latter takes more deliberate and intentional efforts.

Living and Leading Commitment and Accountability
TOOL PRACTICE:

Reflect on the section you have just completed.

1. What is your current perspective?

_____

_____

_____

_____

_____

2. How must you shift your perspective to achieve your goal?

_____

_____

_____

_____

_____

3. What leadership prescriptive actions would you take?

_____

_____

_____

_____

_____

CHAPTER FOURTEEN

Growing Personal Awareness and Self-Management

In our experience, most leaders want to do what is right for the organization and its people. However, many leaders miscalculate their impact trusting that their good intentions will shine through. When this approach fails, they often insist that it was not their intention, and others should understand. Successful leaders react to such miscalculations quite differently; they not only accept ownership for their intention but their impact, as well.

At the core of the leadership tool, *Growing Personal Awareness and Self-Management* is the ability to be clear about what they intend and to own their impact — even in those instances where their intentions were quite different. The former requires self-awareness; the latter requires self-management.

There are several foundational talents and abilities required to use this tool effectively:

- Continually grow in self-awareness by seeking and embracing feedback.
- Hold oneself accountable for one's impact on others.
- Ensure tighter linkages between intentions and impact.

COACHING TIPS

DIAL INTO	DIAL-UP	DIAL-DOWN
Accountability for personal impact: How do you demonstrate that?	Ownership of your impact — whatever your intention.	Rationalizations and excuses.
Self-awareness and your intentions: Do you have a process for understanding when you missed on your intention?	Feedback and coaching that can help you increase your level of self-awareness.	Voices that suggest that "other peoples' feelings, feedback are wrong."
Are you committed to building a tighter linkage between your intent and your impact?	Time to reflect before you act to ensure the linkage between your intent and impact.	Reactions in both thought and words.

DAVID'S STORY

The Choice to Lead

David had a sense of adventure, a tendency to tolerate risk well, and impulses to seize potential opportunities. He enjoyed playing roles that allowed him to operate independently and creatively. When a large global company decided to spin off a division and "re-start" as a separate business, David was among the first to volunteer for the new company. He volunteered for an ill-defined role as "troubleshooter" — to any area needing immediate attention, intervention or general fixing. His first assignment was to manage the sales recruitment team. The salesforce was losing more people than recruiters were able to hire, but the recruitment team did not see any reason to change their methods. Despite his genuine intention to help, the group heard all of his new ideas as invalidating their established practices. They quickly dismissed all of his creative ideas and coaching.

David recognized that although his creativity was an asset, his tendency toward independence was not. His team required clarity, compelling reasons to change, and frequent coaching. He also recognized that if he did not change the thinking of the existing recruitment team, they would not whole-heartedly implement his creative ideas for recruitment and retention. He disciplined himself to spend quality time with his teams, helping them understand why changing conditions dictated new ways of doing things, how innovative approaches would work, and what it meant for them. He was never critical of their past methods and focused on the different conditions they were facing due to business uncertainty. Through his efforts, recruitment surpassed attrition within four weeks, and he quickly gained the support of a committed team.

Leveraging "Hidden Talents"

David was a naturally independent thinker and operator — style that which worked for him early in his career. He became well regarded for his initiative and for his ability to solve problems creatively and quickly without asking for permission. However, as his span of responsibilities widened, his actions touched and affected more individuals outside of his workgroup. He received feedback that his rapid-fire creative suggestions were having an unintended impact on others — leaving them feeling "wrong" for what they previously accomplished and feeling that he was "expedient" in his reactions.

David changed his perspective from "what he wanted to say" to "how he wanted to be heard by others." He trained himself to be more intentional about the words he spoke and the actions he took. He also learned to pause and check-in with others to ensure that his impact, both in words and actions, matched his intent. David accepted ownership for his impact and prescribed measures to ensure that his leadership was received as he intended.

It Starts with Perspective

David changed his perspective, designed a prescription that enabled him to find his hidden talents, remedy his problem, and reach new leadership performance heights.

DAVID'S PERSPECTIVE SHIFT

> Become a leader whose intent and impact consistently match.

LEADERSHIP PRESCRIPTION

> Quiet personal voices that dismiss others' feelings of hurt or disappointment in me.

> Practice clarifying intent before jumping into actions or reactions.

> Set up coaching and feedback network to help me increase self-awareness and self-management.

PERFORMANCE

> Through his efforts, recruitment surpassed attrition within four weeks, and David earned the support of a committed team.

One More Note About David

David chose to become a leader whose intent and impact consistently matched. He grew so much in his self-awareness that he discovered that he had a dream — to be the Chief Human Resources Officer of a company. David is currently living that dream.

OVER AND UNDER-EMPHASIS ON THIS TOOL

When Too Much Emphasis is on Growing Personal Awareness and Self-Management

Some leaders are highly scripted. They carefully analyze their word choice before speaking and may even conduct meetings by reading their carefully crafted notes. They are so concerned about their impact that they miss the personal connection in their delivery and often come across as inauthentic. Feedback from their ecosystem suggests that these leaders appear inauthentic and lacking personal connection.

> ***Does this sound like you or someone you are coaching?***
> *We cannot overestimate how important it is for you to be your authentic self. Carefully crafted messages can just as quickly land unintentionally as those that are spontaneous. The goal is for you to hone your skills and find this right balance. It is better to check in with your "audience" to see if you are landing as you intend than to be overly scripted before you begin.*

When Too Little Emphasis is on Growing Personal Awareness and Self-Management

Some leaders are more inclined to follow their impulses and to react when opportunities present themselves than to take the time to reflect on the situation before responding. They are energized by seizing the moment and by having an immediate impact. Their bias for action is an admirable skill, but there are times when it may create unintended consequences in the environment, such as not having the impact that they intend to have.

> ***Does this sound like you or someone you are coaching?***
> *Likely, following your impulses has always served you well.*

However, as your scope of responsibilities increases, you must be more mindful of the impact your behavior is having on the system around you. We encourage you to slow down your reactions a bit, consider those around you and how your responses might land on them before committing to words or actions. When in doubt, you can always "process check" and ask others how they regarded your words or actions.

FINAL TIP

Reacting and Responding?

When we speak about someone's **reactions**, we are thinking about impulsive, automatic behaviors. Sometimes peoples' reactions are influenced by memories of similar experiences from their past. When we speak about someone's **responses**, we are thinking about actions that one has reflected on and considered. We encourage you to slow down and reflect long enough to ensure that your intentions match the impact of your actions. If your "reactions" are not serving you well, consider some common-sense remedies such as "sleeping on it," going for a walk to clear your head or filing your email response in the "draft" file.

We encourage you to slow down and reflect long enough to ensure that your intentions match the impact of your actions. If your "reactions" are not serving you well, consider some common-sense remedies such as "sleeping on it," going for a walk or filing your email response in the "draft" file.

Growing Personal Awareness And Self-Management
TOOL PRACTICE:

Reflect on the section you have just completed.

1. What is your current perspective?

_____

_____

_____

_____

_____

2. How must you shift your perspective to achieve your goal?

_____

_____

_____

_____

_____

3. What leadership prescriptive actions would you take?

_____

_____

_____

_____

_____

CHAPTER FIFTEEN

Adapting To The Unpredictable Workplace

Leaders in today's workplace are challenged to keep up with the breakneck speed of change. Successful individuals must be more adaptable, flexible, and resourceful. More information is readily available than ever before, and the hunger for this information and data has become insatiable. However, many companies have not yet developed the capabilities to effectively deal with this onslaught and leverage it to make better business decisions. Many leaders wonder along with T. S. Eliot: "Where is the wisdom we have lost in knowledge? Where is the knowledge we have lost in information?"

A common area of frustration for many in today's workplace is the redundant data and information requests that emanate from those more senior and are disruptive to their organizational priorities and workflow. Ironically, the same leaders who make these requests are often those who instruct their direct reports to "get out of those details" and "become more strategic." This practice of distracting "fire drills" will probably continue, but resourceful and adaptive leaders must find ways to soften the impact of this practice.

At the core of the leadership tool, **Adapting to the Unpredictable Workplace** is the resourcefulness and commitment to minimize organizational distractions.

There are several foundational talents and abilities required to use this tool effectively:

- Develop a keen sense for organizational workflow and patterns of the organization.
- Provide the leadership and plan for likely distractions.
- Minimize the impact of the distractions.

COACHING TIPS

DIAL INTO	DIAL-UP	DIAL-DOWN
Organizational Awareness: How well do you understand and can predict workflow, timing, and process patterns?	Notice patterns, rhythm, and dynamics of the organization.	The tendency to ignore organizational clues about patterns, rhythm, and dynamics.
Personal accountability: What can you do to eliminate some surprise distractions?	• Your resourcefulness and adaptability. • Your willingness to "lead from where you are" to solve this problem.	• The tendency toward "it's not my job." • Blaming and complaining.
Who can best help to minimize distractions?	• Tasks or work products that are required. • Accountable individuals to enroll.	Limiting the scope of help to just your silo.

MONICA'S STORY

The Choice to Lead

Many organizations suffer from some degree of "fire drill anxiety" or the anxiety created by last-minute requests that create significant disruption across organizations. While others grew frustrated, Monica drew upon her resourcefulness. Monica figured out how to anticipate the "fire drills," plan for them, and isolate their impact. When she became the executive assistant for one of the C Suite officers, she recognized that "corporate fire drills" affected the productivity of others throughout her organization, so she was determined to become the "conscience for the productivity" of the organization and find a way to minimize the impact of "fire drills." She had a keen sense for the organization's workflow, cadence, and a steady finger on the pulse of the organization, so she could anticipate fire drills well before they occurred. She learned to recognize patterns in these activities, noted them in her calendar, and suggested that others do the same. She built a network of peers, kept them informed, and always ready to distribute the work efficiently among themselves to absorb what could have been disruptive to the entire organization. Monica had so finely-honed these skills that her organization was usually "fire drill" anxiety-free.

Leveraging "Hidden Talents"

Monica was very aware of her external environment. She noticed the workflows in the organization and the patterns that occurred at various times and under different circumstances. She paid attention to the signs that "something was brewing" in the organization from the questions leaders were asking, the meetings they were having, and the organization's "energy." What did not come naturally to her was teaching and leveraging others. She would instead have done "it" herself, but the "it" was too much for her to do. However, over time, she adjusted her perspective from "personal assistant" to "leader of productivity" for the organization. The outcomes she set for herself required that she bring forth new. She devoted time and energy to helping others notice those same workflow patterns and timetables, so they could better anticipate the "fire drills" and create organization channels for getting work completed as efficiently and effectively as possible. Over time, she developed her supporting network and channels that she engaged for distinct kinds of support. She became a great teacher and leader within her organization, and all were grateful for her judgment, her instincts, her planning, and her support.

It Starts with Perspective

Monica changed her perspective, designed a prescription that enabled her to find her hidden talents, remedy her problem, and reach new leadership performance heights.

MONICA'S PERSPECTIVE SHIFT

> Become a leader of productivity who made the unexpected seem routine.

LEADERSHIP PRESCRIPTION

> Reflect on what surprise "fire drills" I can better anticipate — what are the signs, what are the timing patterns?

> Proactively determine a network of support who can most efficiently and effectively address these fire drills.

> Lead through anticipation, communication, facilitation, and oversight.

PERFORMANCE

> She achieved this goal and went on to lead more initiatives to improve organizational efficiency and effectiveness.

One More Note About Monica

Monica chose to become a leader who made the unexpected seem routine. She achieved this goal and went on to take on more and more initiatives to improve organizational efficiency and proficiency. She became well regarded and enjoyed remarkable success as a leader who always "led from wherever she was."

OVER AND UNDER-EMPHASIS ON THIS TOOL

When Too Much Emphasis is on Adapting to the Unpredictable Workplace

When leaders put too much emphasis on **Adapting to the Unpredictable**, they become unpredictable themselves. When they prioritize, they use invisible criteria that others cannot follow. They may be organizationally aware and reacting well to what they see in their ecosystem but, to others, they appear random, ad hoc, disorganized, and unpredictable. It may be tough for the employees of these individuals to follow their lead and anticipate their priorities. These tendencies become particularly problematic as priorities change, sometimes regularly, leaving employees with no structure or established criteria to help them gauge their bosses' expectations. Feedback from their ecosystem typically suggests that these leaders are "all over the place," and "tough to follow." Does this sound like you or someone you are coaching?

> *Does this sound like you or someone you are coaching?*
> *Employees will not be productive and will not take risks if they lack any structure, criteria, or context. We encourage you to select a tool from the excellent quality prioritization tools available (i.e., the Eisenhower Model) and use it with your employees to establish some rules for prioritization to guide them in their frequently changing workplace. The Eisenhower Model is simple, clear, and very adaptable.*

When Too Little Emphasis is on Adapting to the Unpredictable Workplace

In many cases, hierarchy and the high visibility of the request drive work prioritization — especially of the unexpected. Some leaders allow work to flow almost unfiltered into their organizations if a more senior individual originated the request. Feedback from their ecosystem typically suggests that these leaders "do not push back on management," and they "just do it."

Does this sound like you or someone you are coaching? Although prioritizing by the hierarchy or the visibility of the work may appear to be the safest route to take, it is frequently not in the best interests of the business enterprise. An important question to ask is, "what priority is the most important for advancing the full business interests?" Once this task is assigned or in progress, look for diverse ways to handle the other work that remains in scope — delegate, re-negotiate deadlines or plan to complete later. Finally, good leaders learn to distinguish when it is in the best interests of the business to push back on disruptions, hold to their priorities, and re-negotiate deadlines.

FINAL TIP

"The And"

Do you want to introduce new ways to challenge your team and your colleagues to raise the level of their thinking and to generate more creative possibilities? Minimize the use of the word "or" and replace it with the word "and." This simple tip can cut through many of the "false dilemmas" created by individuals, as they attempt to prioritize their work. Individuals create many "false dilemmas" that are perspective limiting. For example, "We can finish this project today *or* this other project today" leads to a choice. Reframed as "We need to finish this project *and* that project today. How do we do that?" The latter can lead to creative thinking and team problem-solving. We encourage you to practice reframing the thinking about your team and avoid "false dilemmas" created by the word "or." The next time you and your team face unexpected distractions, try replacing the choice created by the word "or" with the possibility enabled by the word "and."

Do you want to immediately introduce new ways to challenge your team and your colleagues to raise the level of their thinking and to generate more creative possibilities? Minimize the use of the word "or" and replace it with the word "and."

Adapting To The Unpredictable Workplace
TOOL PRACTICE:

Reflect on the section you have just completed.

1. What is your current perspective?

_____

_____

_____

_____

_____

2. How must you shift your perspective to achieve your goal?

_____

_____

_____

_____

_____

3. What leadership prescriptive actions would you take?

_____

_____

_____

_____

_____

CHAPTER SIXTEEN

Building And Leading Autonomous Teams

Autonomy is a popular topic for discussion in the workplace. Autonomy can be a potent energizer, giving leaders the authority to design their work and perform in a manner that brings out their very best. Knowing that they are performing at their best levels, motivates leaders to strive for even more.

Few leaders are willing builders of team autonomy. Such leaders do not serve their organizations, their teams, or themselves very well. There is always risk inherent in letting go — but if leaders do not have teams capable of operating more and more independently, they do not have the right team members for today's workplace. In either case, the accountability rests with the leader — step back or hire individuals who you trust and will inspire you to step back.

At the core of the leadership tool, **Building and Leading Autonomous Teams** is the willingness and ability to teach others to be successfully independent.

There are several foundational talents and abilities required to use this tool effectively:

- Have the courage to step back from doing the work of the organization.
- Understand the short and long-term skill requirements for your team.

- Coach for development and independence.
- Hold self and team accountable for commitments — both results and development commitments.

COACHING TIPS

DIAL INTO	DIAL-UP	DIAL-DOWN
Self-coaching: What will it take for you as the leader to be willing to step back?	Your reasons to step back.	Your reasons to stay in control.
Team Coaching: What will it take from your team for you to be willing to step back?	• Augmenting your skills as a development coach. • Augmenting the skills of your team.	• The tendency to manage rather than to coach them. • The tendency to coach for performance only — and not for development.

DANTE'S STORY

The Choice to Lead

When Dante's manager decided that he was ready for additional responsibilities and suggested adding the recruitment department to his already busy role, he immediately saw a need to adapt his leadership style. Dante was an independent operator who always sought to build within his team that same autonomy he so enjoyed. He understood that building team autonomy would take time and work. However, Dante decided to make a significant initial investment of time and energy within his newly combined teams. With their input, Dante developed clear objectives. He observed each team member, expanding their responsibilities and focused his coaching on the goals and not the means to those goals. When Dante knew each team member well enough, they developed actionable development plans together. As he saw the patterns of their performance over time, he loosened or tightened his oversight guidelines as required. Each member came along in a unique way and at a different rate, but Dante flexed with their needs and developed a great deal of autonomy among all team members. Within six months, his team was operating at a level of independence that allowed Dante to focus his efforts on the more complex and strategic aspects of his role while enjoying increases in employee satisfaction and commitment.

Leveraging "Hidden Talents"

Dante's natural inclination was always toward managing a more structured process on his team even though he preferred operating independently. Through the years, he developed an excellent ability to trust his team and to build his team members' independence and autonomy. Early in his career, he was known for his precision and his accuracy. As his portfolio of account-abilities expanded, he very painfully learned to delegate; and, he learned to do that from the best possible coaches — his direct reports. Regularly, they collaborated about what he was doing that they could be doing with his support, and the team made those adjustments. As he grew comfortable with the patterns of their performance over time, he loosened or tightened the guidelines for each as required.

Additionally, he clarified goals and objectives with instructions that he relaxed over time. Dante noticed that the time he had available for long-term priorities steadily increased, so he decided to take the next step with his team. As they grew more confident and skilled, and he loosened the oversight guidelines more and more, they became more energized, and their productivity increased. As they grew more successful in their autonomy, so did Dante. For the first time, he received feedback that he was "playing in all the right places." Dante changed his leadership perspective to value team autonomy, made behavioral choices, and became a masterful leader of team autonomy.

It Starts with Perspective

Dante changed his perspective, designed a prescription that enabled him to find his hidden talents, remedy his problem, and reach new leadership performance heights.

DANTE'S PERSPECTIVE SHIFT

> Become a leader who ensures his team's autonomy.

LEADERSHIP PRESCRIPTION

> Quiet inclinations to supervise or manage day-to-day.
>
> Set clear stretch objectives closely aligned with the strategic business plan.
>
> Ensure the right talent — hire and coach for development.

PERFORMANCE

> He achieved his goal and was hugely successful in his new role with expanded responsibilities.

One More Note About Dante

Dante chose to become a leader who ensured the team's autonomy. He achieved his goal and was hugely successful in his new role with expanded responsibilities. His career progressed through a series of expanded responsibilities at higher organizational levels at different companies. He is still especially well regarded for his ability to build autonomous teams.

OVER AND UNDER-EMPHASIS ON THIS TOOL

When Too Much Emphasis is on Building and Leading Autonomous Teams:

Some leaders model their teams after consulting firms. Each member has an independent portfolio of clients or projects; each one has a specialty area and is called into projects as support is required. Beyond that, there is limited interaction within the team and with its leader because the team leader also has his or her portfolio. Feedback from their ecosystem typically suggests that these leaders are "not leading, developing, or building their team."

> *Does this sound like you or someone you are coaching? Reframe your thinking about your responsibilities from "a leader who encourages independence" to "a leader who builds autonomy"—the former assumes self-sufficiency, while the latter builds and nurtures it. Unless you do, it will be difficult for you to hear and act on the feedback you are receiving. One of your most critical roles is to build a team capable of functioning with autonomy but continually growing from your coaching and leadership. If you doubt your coaching skills in this area, seek help.*

When Too Little Emphasis is on Building and Leading Autonomous Teams:

Some leaders are more inclined to manage than lead. They allow little if any, freedom to act, check their employees' work regularly and tend to assign tasks rather than areas of accountability. They permit little, if any, leeway to operate and likely little freedom to decide. Typically, they receive feedback that they are over-managing their team and that their team is over-focused on avoiding risk and under-focused on creativity or innovation. Feedback from their ecosystem typically suggests that these leaders are "stifling innovation" and are "not powerful development leaders."

Does this sound like you or someone you are coaching?
You may be producing perfect results, but is your team learning and growing? Are you learning anything from them? Are they delivering any results they can claim as their own or are they merely assisting you? Is your team producing any innovations? If not, it is probably time to seek coaching from your direct reports. Ask them a few key questions:

- *What is it that they need from you to enable their growth?*
- *What do they need more from you?*
- *What do they need less from you?*
- *What should you continue doing for them that you are already doing?*

FINAL TIP

Delegation and Assigning Tasks?

When we speak of good *"delegators,"* we are thinking about leaders who create a context within their team so that employees can understand their contribution to the bigger picture of the business. They identify impactful, measurable goals, and then they support their employees as needed to run without organizational interference. Leaders who have perfected the art of delegation most often see productivity increases due to the employee's connection to the purpose, values, and mission of the organization. When we speak of leaders who **assign tasks**, we are thinking about leaders who assign more random, isolated, activity-based tasks that they fail to connect to the broader business context. Consider spending time at staff meetings discussing the critical priorities of the business and how your team's objectives and contributions link to them. If you are still inclined to assign random tasks, we suggest that you are likely "doing" too much of the organization's work rather than delegating effectively to your team.

Reframe your thinking about your responsibilities from a leader who encourages independence to a leader who builds autonomy — the former assumes self-sufficiency, while the latter builds and nurtures it.

Building And Leading Autonomous Teams
TOOL PRACTICE:

Reflect on the section you have just completed.

1. What is your current perspective?

_____

_____

_____

_____

_____

2. How must you shift your perspective to achieve your goal?

_____

_____

_____

_____

_____

3. What leadership prescriptive actions would you take?

_____

_____

_____

_____

_____

TOOLS IN COMBINATION
IDENTIFY THE TOOLS USED
IN THIS STORY

"A leader takes people where they want to go. A great leader takes people where they don't necessarily want to go but need to be."

ROSALYN CARTER

When the board decided to spin-off and take a division of a large multi-national company public, the future for the new company did not look bright. There was too much cost, and the growth agenda was only apparent for 18 months. In short, it was a risky venture. From the moment of the announcement, the tension across the organization was almost palpable. The disruption inherent in separating these two entities affected every department in the enterprise. Without the shelter of the larger company and its seemingly unlimited resources, departments that previously had not pulled their weight were suddenly carefully scrutinized, and people were anxious about their futures.

The CEO recognized the need to focus the full attention of the organization on the whole business enterprise while optimizing the segments and the departments[1]. Before the official launch of the new company, he coached his leaders to reframe their experience as a division into a new vision — that of an independent company. He won their confidence by demonstrating his commitment to the future of the company. He did this by leading the creation of corporate values and involving leaders across the company in the strategic planning process. He conducted roadshows, including all the officers of the new company, and they visited every segment and region of the business. The people saw and interacted with their leaders, and their leaders learned more about the needs and dynamics of the business segments and functions.

Meanwhile, Dolce, Senior Vice President of Human Resources, was flooded with transfer requests from people within the division designated to spin with the new company who wanted to stay within the safer "mother ship." Others who were identified to remain with the "mother ship" wanted to become part of the new company. It seemed that no one was where they wanted to be.

Dolce recommended that the new company commit to fielding "a volunteer army," made up of only those employees who wanted to join the spin-off and take the inherent risk. *Dolce recognized that it was essential to build an employee base of committed followership*[2] as the new company embarked on a likely perilous journey. She also believed that the best way to provide what employees needed to commit to the organization was to allow them to choose between the two companies.

The recommendation was accepted. The CEO held the HR team accountable for honoring and advancing the transfer requests that they received. It was easier to find jobs in the large parent company for the "transfer outs;" in fact, many of the "transfer ins" found themselves in roles that were outside of their comfort zone because the parent company had instilled the value of perfection into its employees. That standard had to be reframed in the hearts and minds of these new company employees into *"good enough work" standard — as work that achieves all specifications and quality standards*[3].

The new company enjoyed more success than was initially anticipated. At the root of the early success was the *commitment and accountability*[4] that were seeded and cultivated at the very formation of the company. Employees quickly learned that *doing what they committed and helping others to do the same* were the most highly regarded values in the initial stages of the new company. They enjoyed some exciting rewards in return for their behavior.

This story of the early days of the new company offers a valuable lesson — that **these critical leadership tools, when used in combinations, can be even more impactful than when used in isolation**.

Which "leadership tools" were demonstrated in this story? How did they work together to solve the problem of creating the people team for a new company? *(Answers are below)*.

Answers

[1]Lead while Maximizing for the Business Enterprise; [2]Building Followership through Empathy; [3]Valuing "Good Enough" Work; [4]Living and Leading Commitment and Accountability

A FINAL MESSAGE
FROM THE AUTHORS

The leaders we introduced in this book embraced the practice of shifting their perspective to broaden the scope of their choices and enhance their leadership performance. ***By doing so, they created the opportunity to author new stories for themselves and those around them by discovering and displaying their "hidden talents."*** In some cases, they became so proficient at these skills, they were able to perform them automatically and even unconsciously, while others ***were*** still working to develop them. As a result, each enjoyed enormous success driven by the continued growth and development associated with discovering and employing latent skills and capabilities.

We were proud to introduce you to each of these exceptional leaders as they demonstrated the "sought after and hard to explain" leadership tools available to each of us if we chose to discover and leverage our "hidden talents." John Quincy Adams said, *"If your actions inspire others to dream more, learn more, do more and become more, you are a leader."* The individuals you just met through these chapters lived up to this definition and are authentic leaders.

By reading this book, you have taken an excellent first step. Hopefully, you discovered some of your own "hidden talents." We encourage you to continue to reflect on these leadership stories and the tools they illustrate. Select those that appear most relevant and commit to practicing them in your world.

Now, take the next step in your leadership journey. Allow yourself to "dream more, learn more, do more, and become more" as you reflect upon the stories of these leaders, and as you practice the tools in the book.

Choose to lead and write your own story.

About the Authors

Maryanne DiMarzo is a trailblazer. After a career in higher education and 15 years in human resources, she left corporate life, retiring from Avaya, one of America's leading technology companies, as Chief Human Resources Officer. She is widely acknowledged for her leading-edge human resources leadership, especially her ability to deliver business results through contemporary leadership development practices, featured in a white paper co-authored with Lore Institute titled, *The Leadership Challenge, Accelerating Organizational Transformation Through Leadership Development*. Additionally, she is the author of *Writing Human Software*, a chapter in a book titled, *Human Capital Management*, a 2004 publication dedicated to business impacting human resources leadership. She holds a master's degree from Manhattanville College and a bachelor's degree from Rosemont College. Maryanne formed **Beacon People Solutions** in 2007 with colleague and friend, **Amy Acker**. Shortly after that, Maryanne introduced herself to the world of psychological type and merged those principles with her own beliefs regarding the extraordinary and unique potential of all individuals in business and their lives. Maryanne presents her work in the firm's debut book, **HIDDEN TALENTS**, in which she describes real-life scenarios of leaders who achieve aspirational levels of performance by discovering and developing their leadership talents.

Amy Acker has always had her eyes on the ball. A graduate of Pace University class of 1988 with a degree in Human Resources Management, she attended Pace on a basketball scholarship where she was a two-time Academic All-American. Amy went on to graduate in 1992 with an MBA in Strategic Management and Planning, also from Pace. In 1996, Amy was recruited to join Lucent Technologies, where she began as a senior human resources generalist. In 1998 she became the Director of Human Resources for New Ventures dedicated to incubating start-up businesses for Lucent Technologies. In 2000, Lucent announced their separate enterprise business now known as Avaya. She was asked to join the executive team as one of the founding vice presidents and was named the Vice President of Global Talent Management. A dedicated philanthropist, Amy was formerly President of the non-profit organization Association for Psychological Type International, and currently serves as President of the Indian River Impact 100. In 2007 Amy co-founded the prestigious consulting agency **Beacon People Solutions**. In her spare time, you'll find Amy working in her garden. And, she is still practicing her jump shots.

Rodica Ceslov is a trusted advisor to client executives and startup founders. Previously, she led an award-winning marketing communications firm serving clients spanning technology, consumer products, publishing, healthcare, and nonprofit. She was selected to the Top 100 Small Business CEO's for the New York Region by SmartCEO Magazine. Additionally, she served as president of a non-profit and has been a guest lecturer at colleges in the New York area. In her spare time, she enjoys chess, hiking, and flying.

www.ingramcontent.com/pod-product-compliance
Lightning Source LLC
Chambersburg PA
CBHW050506210326
41521CB00011B/2342